THE ATTRACTIONS OF THE WORLD TO COME.

BY

ALFRED BRYANT,

PASTOR OF THE FIRST PRESBYTERIAN CHURCH, NILES, MICHIGAN.

NEW YORK:
M. W. DODD, PUBLISHER,
No. 506 BROADWAY.
1867.

DEDICATORY.

TO THE CHURCHES IN THE WEST ESPECIALLY, TO WHICH HE HAS PREACHED, AND TO THE PEOPLE AMONG WHOM HE HAS LABORED IN THE GOSPEL, AS WELL AS TO ANY, IN EVERY PLACE, INTO WHOSE HANDS IT MAY FALL, WHO DESIRE A BETTER PORTION THAN EARTH, OR LOVE TO CONTEMPLATE THE FUTURE, THIS WORK IS AFFECTIONATELY INSCRIBED, IN THE HOPE THAT IT MAY CONVINCE THE DOUBTING—RECLAIM THE WANDERING—GUIDE THE ERRING—COMFORT THE AFFLICTED—CHEER THE DESPONDING—AND LEAD SOME TO SEEK MORE EARNESTLY THE BLESSINGS OF ETERNAL LIFE.

Contents.

CHAPTER III.

THE INTERMEDIATE STATE.

CHAPTER IV.

THE RESURRECTION.

CHAPTER V.

THE DAY OF JUDGMENT.

CHAPTER VI.

THE NATURE OF FUTURE HAPPINESS.

CHAPTER VII.

THE NATURE OF FUTURE PUNISHMENT.

CHAPTER I.

INTRODUCTORY.

"Earth has engrossed my love too long,
'Tis time I lift my eyes
Upward, Dear Father, to thy throne,
And to my native skies."

WITH those who believe that we are created for, and destined to another and a higher life than the present, there can be no question where our affections ought to be placed, and for what we ought to live. Our days on earth are as a hand-breadth. Life is a vapor, which endureth for a little time, and then passes away. We are like grass—"in the morning it flourisheth, and groweth up; in the evening it is cut down, and withereth." Even the generations of men chase one another in rapid succession, as shadows o'er the plain, and continue not. How poor a thing is human life in itself considered. It is the future only,—man's immortal destiny,—which gives worth and dignity to his existence. It seems a folly, therefore, exceedingly stupid, to be so in love and taken up with the present, as to neglect the future world.

True wisdom dictates a different course. We

should live for the highest end of our being. Casting our eyes prospectively along the vista of those eternal ages, through which we are successively to pass, we should aim so to live, that in the present we might lay the sure foundation for our highest welfare in the life to come.

What folly it would be in youth to be so captivated with momentary pleasures as to neglect that education which was essential to fit them for the business, the usefulness, and enjoyment of manhood's maturer years. In what light, then, shall we regard that course of thought, action, and pursuit, which is blind to the future world, and which disregards the influence our present existence is to have on that to which we are destined? There is a strange infatuation in human minds. The things of time and sense, which are so transient and illusory so captivate and enchant, that the world to come, for which we were made, and to which we are hastening, is, for the most part, wholly obscured.

This is one of the sad and darkening effects of sin. It dims, or puts out the vision of faith in things unseen. It practically blots out a future existence —turns man away from God, a wretched wanderer —and the bright and glorious destiny for which he was made. It leads him to seek and love the creature more than God the Creator, who is over all, blessed forever.

Under the influence of a mind darkened and bewildered in respect to spiritual things, the tendency of all things earthly is away from God, and that life of faith, which is designed to prepare us for those transformations, which are to usher us into those brighter spheres in reserve, in the undeveloped future. And yet the world to come was never more a reality, or nearer, or more important, than at present. The dark river of death rolls its turbid waters continually onward, carrying away, as with a flood, man and his works. Along its banks "wisdom crieth! She uttereth her voice in the streets: she crieth in the chief place of concourse, in the opening of the gates: in the city she uttereth her words, saying, How long, ye simple ones, will ye love simplicity? and the scorners delight in their scorning, and fools hate knowledge? Turn you at my reproof: behold, I will pour out my spirit unto you; I will make known my words unto you." "Set your affections on things above, and not on things on the earth." "Seek first the kingdom of God, and his righteousness." But how generally is the voice of heavenly wisdom lost amid the excitement, the anxieties, and the giddy whirl of life.

The dangers of a supreme and all-absorbing worldliness, to the exclusion of eternal things, were never greater than at the present day. The marvellous inventions and improvements, and discoveries of the present age, have given an unwonted impetus to the human mind, and sent it forth amid intense excitement, into new and untried fields of worldly enterprise and adventure. It is almost impossible not to let go heaven, and join in the onward rush for wealth, pleasure and glory. Were all these influences setting heavenward, the prospect would be glorious and holy; but they run, for the most part, in an opposite direction. There is even danger that the various benevolent institutions, which are regarded as the glory of the age, will become animated by the same worldly spirit, and be regarded chiefly as valuable, on account of their ameliorating influence on man as a citizen of earth, and not on account of their tendency to prepare him, as an immortal being, for an unending life.

On the well-established principle, that the present age is mainly decisive of that which is next to come, the indications are, that the time coming will be one of unparalleled wealth and splendor, and of concentrated worldliness in all its sensual and earth-loving forms. If it is not so, it will be because the danger is averted by stronger spiritual influences than are now put forth—by a more intense and devoted heavenly mindedness in the church, and a warmer love for things unseen than is now manifest.

It is becoming, therefore, for each one in his sphere, to labor to give to eternal things their true prominence, and to urge their claims on human attention and love. Such is the professed design of the following pages.

It is an exceedingly erroneous idea, too commonly entertained, that the realities of the world to come are only gloomy and repulsive; and that strong and steadfast views of a future life are joyless, and unsuited to the necessary duties, pursuits, and enjoyments of the present world. But this is a great mistake. Error, delusion, and fanaticism, may render any world dark and forbidding by their distorted and extravagant representation; but truth, from the pure fountain, beaming as light from the sun, clothes all in beauty. When orderly and scripturally contemplated, the future world has attractions infinitely surpassing any objects or glories which earth can present, and powers to elevate, ennoble and refine the soul, and fill it with joy unspeakable, which no agencies beneath the Unseen can exert.

There is an occasional, unwilling, and imperfect view of the realities of an endless life, which is indeed gloomy enough, as it is forced upon the mind by disease or death, in the midst of worldly prosperity and sin. And there is sometimes on the part of the wicked, a fearful looking for of judgment, which renders the whole subject of a future state repulsive. But it need not be so to any who "do justly, love mercy, and walk humbly with God."

Why should not the world to come, be to the good especially, transcendently attractive? The Creator has certainly sought to render it so, in all the delineations of his word. It is presented to us as his own peculiar dwelling-place, where he will unveil himself, and manifest his glories, in visions more resplendent and enduring than have ever been conceived on earth. It is the world to which Jesus has gone, and where he ever lives, in his glorified human form. It is described to us as the home of angels, and the abode of the departed, and where the holy experience joys which never weary, and pleasures which are forever more.

Are there no attractions in God? and none in him, who is the brightness of the Father's glory, and the express image of his person? The heavens declare the glory of the Lord, and the firmament showeth forth his handiwork; and this bright and beautiful universe, in which we live, was designed to shadow forth to creatures the attractive loveliness and glories of the Incomprehensible. But O, if things seen, even amid the dim twilight of time, are often so exceedingly lovely and fascinating, what must the great source be from which all spring?

From the beauties and attractions of this present world, we may justly infer the surpassing loveliness and glories of the world to come. This is a lovely world, to any who have a mind sufficiently elevated and refined to enjoy it. How beautiful the mountain, and the valley—the running brook,—the flowing river and the rolling ocean! How pleasant the seasons with all their variations; and how well adapted, in their ever-changing forms to break up the monotony of life, and fill the mind with a succession of pleasurable emotions and contemplations. How kind, too, are the provisions of Providence, and how many are the sources of innocent enjoyment continually opened for our gratification. How sweet, too, is human love to those whose hearts are attuned to harmony and friendship!

We can readily conceive, that were all sin removed from the present world, and those miseries which it has introduced, it might be an Eden—a garden of pleasures even now, which would fill the soul to overflowing. When, therefore, we are taught, that the present world is only designed as preparatory to one to come, far more glorious—the introduction to our immortal existence—the vestibule to the grand and eternal temple of life, into which we are soon to enter—we are justified in the inference, that the future must be far more beautiful and attractive than anything now seen or conceived.

Accordingly, we find it recorded in Scripture, that God has not only commanded us to set our affections on things above, and to seek them in preference to all others; but he has designedly employed those objects and things on earth, most desirable, beautiful, and attractive—as emblems of the glorious attractions and blessedness of the life to come.

Among the things of earth more generally coveted than any other, is wealth. It stands as the representative of all earthly wants, and furnishes the means for those gratifications which are most dear to every one who longs for present pleasure. But riches are here deceitful. They cannot give the bliss for which men sigh, nor satisfy the cravings of an ever-aspiring mind.

Now, to draw men upward, and to lead them to seek that preparation which is essential to the enjoyment of an endless life, God employs riches, great, unfading, and inexhaustible, as an emblem of those never-failing sources of happiness which are laid up in heaven for the holy. The world to come, with the glorious blessedness which pervades it, is represented to us as "*true riches*," as "a *better* and *enduring substance*," as "*an inheritance incorruptible, undefiled, and that cannot fade away*," and as "*treasures which no rust can corrupt, and which no thieves can steal*."

How kindly and tenderly does God here address himself to all the lovers of riches, and how, by coming down to their comprehension, does he seek to invest that future world for which *He* has made them, with those attractions most likely to captivate and lead them away from those vain pursuits which must end in disappointment! Unlike those of the present world, the riches of the future are true, unfading, and ever-enduring. No fires can consume them—no thief steal them, and no exposure through eternity's long ages cause them to fade. In this respect, could the Lord have presented the world to come to us, more attractively?

Honor is also prominent with multitudes, as an object of intense desire. The voice of fame is sc sweet, and enchanting—

> "That many think, to live without her song
> Is rather death than life. To live unknown,
> Unnoticed, unrenowned! to die unpraised,
> Unepitaphed! to go down to the pit,
> And moulder in the dust among vile worms,
> And leave no whispering of a name on earth!—
> Such thought is cold about the heart, and chills
> The blood. Who can endure it? who can choose

> Without a struggle, to be swept away
> From all remembrance, and have part no more
> With living men?"

Hence, in every pursuit and department of life we see men eagerly engaged in seeking this shadowy phantom, and enduring immense toil and sacrifice to secure it.

Now, to shadow forth the glorious attractions of the world to come, and to gain the ear of all who thirst for the honor that cometh from men, God employs *honor* as an emblem of the renowned distinction and reward which will be conferred upon all who love him. It is promised to all such that they shall be "*kings* and *priests unto God, and shall reign with him forever and ever*"—that they shall be introduced to the most honorable and glorious society, and be openly acknowledged and confessed before God and all his angels. Can human minds conceive of honors and distinctions more lofty, captivating or satisfying than are presented in these promises. If earthly fame then can enchant, and the honor of men lure to noble deeds, and to the highest achievements, must not the world to come, according to the representations of Scripture, possess superior attractions in all these respects, and more dazzling glories than gather in vain pomp and show around the courts and palaces of kings? Accordingly, we are repeatedly exhorted to strive for glory and honor, by a faithful continuance in well-doing, and to seek the honor that cometh from God only.

But the great mass of mankind who never rise to distinguished wealth or fame on earth, are intent on pleasure. All desire enjoyment of some kind, and eagerly pursue it as their passions and propensities dictate. To all such God cries, in his Word, "Ho, every one that thirsteth, come ye to the waters. Wherefore do ye spend money for that which is not bread? and your labor for that which satisfieth not? harken diligently unto me, and eat ye that which is good, and let your soul delight itself in fatness. In his presence is fulness of joy, at his right hand are pleasures for evermore."

It is not our object to dwell upon the import of these promises in this connection. It will be the design of the following pages to unfold in order the attractions and powers of the world to come. Reference is made to these things here, simply to show that God has sought, in all the emblematic representations of his Word, to invest the life to come with a loveliness and charm which attach to none of those things most highly prized and intensely sought on earth; and that, therefore, the conclusion is exceedingly erroneous, that it is a joyless and gloomy life to have our affections set upon things above, and to be living continually in reference to these high honors and joys which God has promised. Such a life is enlivened with hopes full of immortal glory, and with prospects of joy unspeakable and unfading.

In view of these things, we are not surprised to learn, from Scripture testimony, that to patriarchs and prophets, the promises and prospects of an immortal life possessed attractions sufficiently strong to overcome their love of earth—to conquer their fear of death, and to arm them with undying energy in their devotion to God, "that they might obtain a better resurrection." In comparison with the better life, which was the great object of their faith, earth had no charms. They "confessed that they were strangers and pilgrims on the earth—that they desired a better country, that is, a heavenly, and looked for a city which hath foundations whose builder and maker is God."

Nor was the contemplation of the world to come, with all its terrors and illuminated glories, as brought to view in the gospel, sad or repulsive to the apostles and primitive Christians. Something of their views and joys may be learned from a few scriptural quotations. Peter says, "Blessed be the God and Father of our Lord Jesus Christ, which, according to his abundant mercy, hath begotten us again unto a lively hope by the resurrection of Jesus Christ from the dead, to an inheritance incorruptible, and undefiled, and that fadeth not away, reserved in heaven for you. who are kept by the power of God through faith unto salvation, ready to be revealed in the last time; wherein ye greatly rejoice, though now for a season, ye are in heaviness through manifold temptations: that the trial of your faith, being more precious than of gold that perisheth, though it be tried with fire, might be found unto praise, and honor, and glory, at the appearing of Jesus Christ: whom having not seen, ye love; in whom, though now ye see him not, yet believing, ye rejoice with joy unspeakable and full of glory, receiving the end of your faith, even the salvation of your souls."

It is manifest from this, that to the apostle and those to whom he wrote, the realities and prospects of the world to come were all joyous, and drew them upward with an attraction which no gravitating power of earth could overcome.

Such, too, were the convictions of Paul, in reference to things unseen, that language seemed inadequate to express his ever-kindling emotions, and enraptured persuasions, in prospect of the wondrous things to be revealed. On different occasions he calls them "*glory*"—"*a weight of glory*"—"*a far more exceeding and an eternal weight of glory.*" In regard to all the advantages and happiness this world could bestow, he declares that he counted them all but dung that he might win Christ, and obtain a better resurrection. "For I reckon," he says, "that the sufferings of this present time are not worthy to be compared with the glory which shall be revealed in us."

And these joyous exultations were common to primitive Christians, and enabled those, who through great tribulation were called to enter the kingdom of God, to rejoice that they were counted worthy to suffer shame for Christ in prospect of a participation in the blessedness of his everlasting kingdom.

These are not the dreams of visionaries, but the

words of truth and soberness. A careful consideration of the revelations of Scripture in reference to this subject, in their order and infinite magnitude, will fully justify the most exulting joy, and the most ardent anticipation of which our natures are capable.

The importance of fixed and abiding views of the world to come, and such a living realization of eternal things, as shall lead us to live and act in reference to them, cannot be over-estimated.

Every thing in religion—everything in respect to our highest happiness, turns upon our belief in, and our realization of a world to come. The gospel is unmeaning without it. As a remedy for sin, it can never be appreciated, and will never be accepted only as it is illuminated by the clear light of eternity, and viewed through an abiding faith in things unseen. Jesus will be precious only to those who believe, and his favor sought only as we expect soon to be with him, and share his glory. Sin will be esteemed an evil of magnitude, only as it is seen in the light of eternal realities, and contemplated in its ruinous consequences through unending duration. The doctrines of repentance, regeneration, sanctification, and every truth of Scripture, derive their power and importance wholly from the world to come. It is only from motives thence derived that any can be moved or persuaded to a religious life, and to follow that holiness, without which no man shall see the Lord. And this, too, is the stalk upon which all true virtue on earth must be engrafted, and by which its life must be sustained. Without it, it will have but a sickly and precarious existence.

There is no person, or class, to whom the world to come does not present attractions surpassingly beautiful and inspiring, if they were but seen in their own living light. But to the sons and daughters of sorrow, especially, they present an effectual antidote for all life's woes. "Blessed is he that readeth and understandeth."

And then, too, unlike the present, the world to come is continually gaining in attractions. What a tide of human beings is setting thither! How many of the great, and the good, and the loved, are constantly going! "Perhaps, thou hast a brother or a sister there; that should draw you towards heaven. Perhaps a mother—she whose eye wept while it watched over thee, until at length it grew dim, and closed. Perhaps one nearer, dearer than child, than brother, than mother,—the nearest, dearest is there. Shall I say who, Christian female? thy husband. Christian father, the young mother of thy babes. *He* is not. *She* is not; for God took them. Has heaven no attractions?"

CHAPTER II.

THE IMMORTALITY OF THE SOUL.

This is the bud of being, the dim dawn,
The twilight of our day, the vestibule.
Life's theatre as yet is shut, and death,
Strong death, alone can heave the massy bar
This gross impediment of clay remove,
And make us embryos of existence free.
From real life, but little more remote
Is he, not yet a candidate for light,
The future embryo, slumbering in his sire.
Embryos we must be till we burst the shell,
Yon ambient azure shell, and spring to life,
The life of Gods, O transport, and of man."

YOUNG.

THE ANXIOUS INQUIRY.

"MAN that is born of a woman is of few days, and full of trouble. He cometh forth like a flower and is cut down: he fleeth also as a shadow, and continueth not." How affectingly truthful and solemn are these words of the inspired. They have lost nothing of their significance or appropriateness through the long lapse of ages. The dark river of death still rolls continuously and ceaselessly onward, and the generations of men are hurried away to that vast, shoreless, unfathomed ocean, whence none return. And how it comes home, as a startling and momentous reality—" If I wait," even to the longest period of human life, " the grave is mine house." Corruption shall be my father, the worm my mother and my sister. "There is no discharge in this war." Not only the old, the decrepid, the friendless, the miserable, for whom earth has no more joys or hopes, must die; but—

> " Our eyes have seen the rosy light
> Of youth's soft cheek decay,
> And fate descend in sudden night,
> On manhood's middle day."

But what follows? When death sunders all the ties of earth, and the grave closes upon us, and upon our friends, and hides us from the gaze or knowledge of the living, are we to see and embrace each other no more? Does life, like an expiring candle, go out in eternal darkness? Long, long ago, the question was propounded with anxious solicitude—if a man die, shall he live again? "There is hope," said the inquirer, " of a tree, if it be cut down, that it will sprout again, and that the tender branch thereof will not cease. Though the root thereof wax old in the earth, and the stalk thereof die in the ground, yet through the scent of water it will bud, and bring forth boughs like a plant. But man dieth and wasteth away: yea man giveth up the ghost, and where is he?"—*Job*, 14 : 7–10. Does he descend to earth, or rise to some spirit land?

Does he cease to exist, or in some disembodied or embodied form, outlive the wreck of his corruptible body, susceptible of pleasure and pain as now, in a new and higher sphere of being?

In every age of the world these, with many, have been questions of deep and anxious interest. But how can they, with certainty, be answered? Beyond the grave we cannot see. An impenetrable veil is before us. With things unseen, and beyond the reach of our senses, we cannot hold converse as we can with things of earth. Heaven designedly and wisely, and no doubt benevolently, has closed our sight and senses to things unseen. How then can we know, that when a man dies, he does or shall live again?

NOT DISCOVERED BY REASON.

It is by no means certain that human reason and learning could ever have given a satisfactory answer independently of revelation. "The evidence which the light of reason and nature throws upon the great realities of the coming world, is indeed amazingly strong. Some of the loftiest minds of antiquity seemed to have a fore-shadowing of these great truths. Their attempts are remarkable, in many respects, as a display of comprehensive intellect, and acute powers of disquisition; but they remain as monuments of the inability of minds, unaided by heavenly wisdom, to grasp the wonders of an unseen life." And then it is more than probable, that their primary ideas respecting another life were derived from Divine Revelation, communicated in the beginning, and which descended to the nations through tradition, and such other agencies as were appointed among his people in the institutions of religion. For, as Lord Bolingbroke acknowledges, "the doctrine of the immortality of the soul, and a future state of rewards and punishments, began to be taught before we have any light into antiquity. And when we begin to have any, we find it established that it was inculcated from times immemorial."

And we find it equally prevalent among the most barbarous, as among the most civilized nations. "The ancient Sythians, Indians, Gauls, Germans, Britons, as well as the Greeks and Romans, believed that souls are immortal, and that men shall live in another state after death, though it must be confessed their ideas of it were often very obscure."—*Leland on Rev.*, vol. ii., pp. 272–275.

It is manifest from all this, that the doctrine of man's immortality is exceedingly old, and runs back beyond the memory of mankind. Whence was it derived? Is there any more reasonable supposition, than from Divine Revelation? It is not disputed, that life and immortality are the great themes of the New Testament Scriptures; but the belief has extensively prevailed, that a future life was but indistinctly known, and dimly shadowed forth during the Old Testament dispensation. But was this the fact? When it is affirmed by the apostle, that Jesus Christ has abolished death, and brought life and immortality to light through the Gospel, 2 *Tim.* 1 : 10, a gréat and glorious truth is undoubtedly uttered. It is only through the gospel that eternal life is revealed to fallen man. The Gospel has been too narrowly interpreted by some, as having reference to the great doctrines and facts brought to view in the New Testament. But the Gospel—the good news of salvation through Jesus Christ, in another life, and the glories of his future and eternal kingdom, was preached, we are assured, to Abraham, *Gal.* 3 : 8, and to the children of Israel in the wilderness, *Heb.* 4 : 2. It was preached to Adam, and to Abel, to Enoch and Noah, to Daniel and Isaiah, to all the saints of old, and to all who might have been saints, from the first promise of a Saviour given to Adam, down through all subsequent revelations.

Of those who lived and died in the faith of the promises of future reward and blessedness given, the Apostle Paul says, *Heb.* 11: 13–16, "They confessed that they were strangers and pilgrims on the earth—that they desired and sought a better country, that is, a heavenly—and that they looked for a city which hath foundation, whose builder and maker is God." And it is furthermore declared, that in all their fiery trials, and in the bitter persecutions waged against them, they would not accept deliverance, "that they might obtain a better resurrection."

It is clear from this, that the Old Testament saints, from the beginning, had as firm a persuasion of a future life, as any now have; and that their views of its exceeding blessedness were so distinct and vivid, as to exert an all-controlling influence over their lives, and to lead them to live continually in expectation of, and preparation for it. It had for them attraction sufficiently beautiful and glorious to draw them upward with a power which no earthly temptations or enjoyments could weaken or destroy.

Life and immortality are the great burden of the gospel whenever and wherever preached. It would indeed have been a strange, and an unaccountable thing, had God left the world in darkness, in regard to that endless life for which man was made, until the time of the advent of our Lord. It would be a sad impeachment of the goodness and wisdom of the Creator, to suppose that he made man immortal, and designed him to prepare in this world for happiness in the future, and yet withheld from him the distinct knowledge of this great and cardinal truth of all religion; or left him to work out the problem of his own existence, through long ages of doubt, by his own feeble and darkened powers.

But of no such folly and unkindness was the Creator guilty, as is manifest not only from Scripture, but from the fact that a belief in another life has existed among all nations from time immemorial.

ITS TRUE ORIGIN.

When God created man, he no doubt communicated to him, in some certain way, the design of his creation, and the destiny of his being. And then all along down through the developments of revelation, he sought by miraculous and supernatural interposition, to give renewed assurance of another and a better life, and to impress it indelibly on the human mind. The great design in the translation of Enoch, a most eminent saint, to the other world, without passing through the gates of the grave, was to give to the world in its infancy, a visible, a living, and miraculous demonstration of the reality of a future life.

And had the Creator, who seeks to draw men to himself, and to the higher destinies of their nature, wished to have impressed this truth most vividly upon the minds of men, how could he have done it more effectually, than by transferring one, towering in goodness above all others, to the regions of the blest, without seeing death?

The translation of one so great and good, would not only furnish a miraculous demonstration of another life; but would intimate to the living, in clearest light, the character required to fit them for an entrance into a happy life.

Enoch was no doubt translated in the presence of witnesses, who saw him go up, as the disciples saw the Saviour, and who would report the wondrous event to others, and they again to others, until it spread the world around, and men everywhere be led to inquire and study respecting another, and a separate state of existence.

The world rolled on in its course after this, and generations came and went; and then to revive and strengthen the impressions heretofore made, God interposed again, with another miraculous demonstration. Elijah, the prophet, eminently devoted and holy, was openly taken up to heaven, while Elisha, the man of God, in wrapt amazement and joy, exclaimed, "My Father! my Father! The chariot of Israel and the horsemen thereof!" 2 *Kings*, 2 : 11, 12.

In those early times, and thence down through succeeding dispensations to the advent of our Lord, the attention of men was strongly and supernaturally called to another world, by the frequent personal appearance and visible manifestation of angels, to bear to men some message of love, or to perform some deed of providence in the execution of Heaven's purpose. These angelic appearances could not but have had a powerful influence in calling attention, and thought, and inquiry to the unseen world. How naturally would men ask, Whence come these angels? and whither do they go? and where is the place of their abode? And thus how irresistibly all these things would suggest and impress the idea of a world to come.

CLEARLY REVEALED IN THE OLD TESTAMENT.

From these considerations it is manifest that there are much clearer revelations of a future life and its wondrous realities, in the writings of Moses and the prophets, than some have supposed. When Dives, as represented in the parable spoken by our Lord, requested Abraham to send Lazarus to his brethren, to warn them lest they also come into that place of torment, Abraham replied, "they have Moses and the prophets; let them hear them. And he said, nay, Father Abraham; but if one went unto them from the dead, they would repent. And he said unto him, If they hear not Moses and the prophets, neither will they be persuaded though one rose from the dead."

This clearly shows that in the estimation of our Lord, the writings of Moses and the prophets abundantly revealed the reality of a future state of rewards and punishments, and were amply sufficient to satisfy any who were willing to be convinced, and to render them inexcusable in disregarding their warnings and required preparations.

Every typical institution, and every sacrifice through which the believer looked to a coming Redeemer and an atoning sacrifice, also directed him, as with the finger of God, to another life beyond the present; for without this great and all-pervading idea, the promises given of a Saviour, and every type referring to him, would have been soulless and unmeaning. Moses, then, and the prophets, are full of the world to come, as they are full of Jesus and redeeming love.

When we come to the New Testament, no one doubts that here life and immortality are clearly and prominently revealed. In the teachings of our Lord, and in his own resurrection and glorious ascension, an illuminated glory is shed upon all the themes of another life, "like another morn risen on mid-noon." The passage which declares that Jesus Christ has abolished death, and brought life and immortality to light through the gospel, probably has a more special reference to the resurrection of the dead, than to the reality of another life. Life and immortality, in respect to the resurrection of the dead, was indeed brought out to the light, when death and hades were led conquered, by a rising and ascending God.

In the foregoing remarks, the object has been to show that the great idea of another and a better life did not originate in the penetration and reason of man, but was from the beginning a revelation from the Being who made us, and whose kindness would not permit him to keep the world in darkness respecting the destiny for which man was created.

But as all truth must be harmonious, and as the realities of a future life, if true, must be in accordance with the nature of man, and with all his rational, moral, and immortal powers, it is easy, when the idea is fully suggested or revealed, to see its entire harmony with the nature and reason of man, and to argue its certainty from many plausible and possible considerations independent of Scripture. The limits assigned to this work will permit only a brief statement of some of the more prominent arguments upon which reliance has been placed.

ARGUMENT FROM UNIVERSAL ASSENT.

1. The immortality of the soul has been argued *from the assent of all nations to its truth.* Though men have differed widely respecting the nature, the employments, and enjoyments of a world to come, it cannot be disputed that the grand idea of the soul's immortality has, with a few exceptions among the more barbarous tribes of Africa, been universally received. And all this shows not only that the mind of man universally is receptive of the full idea of another life, but that it is in harmony with his instinctive nature, or it could not find so ready an admission. But however this general consent may be accounted for, or to whatever source it may be attributed, it certainly forms a strong presumptive argument in favor of a better life. Cicero long since observed; " In everything the consent of all nations is to be accounted the law of nature, and to resist it, is to resist the voice of God."

ARGUMENT FROM LOVE OF EXISTENCE.

2. The immortality of the soul has been argued with great force and plausibility, from man's inward dread naturally of annihilation, and from those longing desires for life, and pleasing hopes, which the idea of a blissful future awakens.

It is true this fond desire, these pleasing hopes,

are not universal. With some who have received unscriptural views of another life, and who have little hope respecting the future, an endless life has no attractions. They would rather lie silently in the grave, than ever awaken to life. And to others whose wickedness leads them to look for a fiery indignation, nothing would be more welcome than an assurance of an entire extinction of their being at death. But it is believed that this is not the common feeling. With most, there is a desire of immortality—an inward longing for a life, higher and better than earth can give. The soliloquy which Addison puts into the mouth of Cato, has force and beauty in it, and is descriptive of a common sentiment:

> "It must be so—Plato, thou reasonest well!
> Else whence this pleasing hope, this fond desire,
> This longing after immortality?
> Or whence this secret dread, and inward horror,
> Of falling into nought? Why shrinks the soul
> Back on herself, and startles at destruction?
> 'Tis the divinity that stirs within us,
> 'Tis heaven itself that points out an hereafter
> And intimates eternity to man."

Has the Creator, then, so constituted the human mind that these strong desires—these pleasing hopes—these earnest longings after a future life, may arise and be indulged only that they may be extinguished in eternal night and disappointment? Or does not rather the fact, that these things are in accordance with the native instincts of the mind, clearly indicate the reality of a life beyond the confines of the grave?

Would wings be folded in the worm, if they were not one day to enable it to fly? Would thought continually reach out into the future, if one day we were not to explore that "dim distant?" Would the heart, at times, be seized with longings not of this earth, if these longings had not a full realization somewhere? How else would the great mystery of human life be solved? What an anomaly man would be, with all his undying aspirations and powers, amid the creatures of God, were he not, in accordance with his nature, immortal?

But not only our love of existence—our longing after immortality—but our anxiety to become acquainted with things which are dimly shadowed forth in the surrounding universe, and which we know to exist, intimates a future life. For example, who that has the least knowledge of astronomy, and whose soul has been kindled by the conjectures which revolving worlds and systems have excited, has not sometimes felt an irrepressible desire to know something more definite of the character of those worlds, of their geography and inhabitants; and the mysterious agencies and laws which are seen at work among them? It is but a little that the wisest now know. Death commonly puts an end to their career, while they are yet upon the very threshold of nature's grand temple of knowledge, and eagerly desiring to look into things unseen. Attraction, gravitation, electricity, magnetism, and the like, are names given to agencies and laws, which elude the grasp of man, and are, in many respects, at present unsearchable. In the simplest things in nature, and in the most common productions, there are mysteries which the learning of ages has not yet been able to solve, but in regard to which every intelligent mind longs to be informed.

Must there not be another life then, when an opportunity will be given to satisfy these desires, and unfold those things upon which our eyes intently gaze for a moment before they are dimmed in death. Can it be, that with these desires for knowing, kindled by God's own works, we sink into nothing when death dissolves our connection with present things? How cruel it would be, thus to deal with man—to place above and around him such wonderful and glorious objects, and to excite such a thirst for knowledge, and then never give the opportunity of knowing—but set him down just as he begins to look, and know, and inquire! It cannot be. Goodness and wisdom forbid it. These indications and yearnings of nature, point with an unerring finger, to a life which never dies—and a career which never terminates. The objector must maintain that life is a great cheat, if this is not so—and that God is capable of playing off upon the human race so great a deception—as to excite desires which are never to be gratified—to enkindle hopes which are never to be realized, and to excite within him immortal instincts which point to no real object and ensure no valuable end.

ARGUMENT FROM INSTINCT.

There is one consideration intimated in what has been said, which is worthy of a more extended consideration. In all the works of God, it cannot be discovered, that he has made anything in vain, when the use and reason of things are understood. Every natural or animal instinct, we know, has an end for which it was designed, and to which it points; and the end therefore of the instinct, or the object it was intended to accomplish, is as certain in its existence, as is the natural and spontaneous principle that implies it.

Thus, in every animal there is an instinct, whether herbivorous or carnivorous, to a particular kind of food, which springs not from reason or education; and a bodily apparatus, most wisely and delicately adjusted, for procuring the food to which the instinct leads. Water fowls have a native instinct for water, and for the food thence to be attained, and everything is provided for and adapted to their instinct. And so through universal nature. As the cold winter draws on, instinct leads most of the feathered tribe to seek a shelter from the blast they could not endure in some warmer and more genial clime. And such a clime exists most benevolently corresponding to their instinctive wants, where a warm sun, and "never-failing spring abides." How beautiful and wise the arrangement. How surely does every native instinct and desire indicate the certain existence of that to which it points. And hence it seems a clear and certain inference, that these pleasing hopes, which spring eternal in the human heart—these longings after immortality,—which the annunciations of an endless life inspire, have their appropriate end, and as surely prove a future life, as any instinct in nature demonstrates the existence of its object. How could the Creator have indicated an hereafter to man more clearly, in the arrangements of nature, than in these desires, and hopes, and aspirations of the human mind?

As the tender bird seeks in a more genial clime a shelter from the cold, and finds it, so will we, who long for some sunny clime away from the wintry storms of life, as surely find the object of our hopes.

ARGUMENT FROM THE POWERS OF MIND.

The immortality of the soul has been often argued from the wonderful powers and capabilities of the human intellect, and its susceptibility of, to us, indefinite improvement. See, for example, what a vast difference there is between the infant and the man of forty or sixty years, in the midst of his career of improvement and fame. What proficiency in knowledge is made, what intellectual grasp is developed during these short years! To what heights of intellectual greatness did Newton, Laplace, Herschell, and hosts of others eminent in the State, and in every department of science, attain during their sojourn on earth! And with more ordinary minds, and a more common zeal, how many things are learned, how much knowledge acquired in the course of life! And there is manifestly no limit to intellectual improvement and development this side the grave, when appropriate effort is made for its accomplishment. Unobstructed by disease or accident, knowledge may be acquired every day, and a man may continue to rise higher and higher in the ever-widening grasp of his expanding mind.

Now give human minds free scope, remove the obstructions of disease and death, place an immortal career before them, and around them God's wonderful works and ways, infinite and incomprehensible, as incentives to thought and study, and who can imagine the greatness of intellectual development and expansion to which they may attain?

They may reach the highest point to which an archangel has ever yet attained; and as the eagle, with his eye resting on the sun, and his wings upon the wind, mounts steadily upward towards the bright orb, till lost in the effulgence of its blaze; so human minds, carreering on beyond where Gabriel now stands or soars in heaven's own light, may in intellectual and moral progress direct their way towards the creative mind, though never able to reach the Infinite. The powers and capabilities of the human mind are wonderful and past finding out, as is manifest in all the discoveries of science, and in all the advancement and inventions of art. And now is it not reasonable to infer that minds so admirably constituted and endowed, must be designed for something higher than this world affords? Is it not in accordance with the wisdom and goodness of God, and with the nature of the human mind, to infer that it is immortal, and destined, according to its capabilities, to an unending career? What an impeachment it would be of the wisdom and goodness of God to suppose that he had created minds, with such vast and inconceivable powers, only that he might dash them, with their frail tabernacles, in pieces at death—that he had lighted up such intellectual lamps, beaming forth, even amid the darkness and obstructions of earth, with surpassing brilliancy and beauty, only that he might quench them in the gloomy night of annihilation.

"How can it enter into the thought of man, that the soul which is capable of such immense perfection, and of receiving new improvements to all eternity, shall fall away into nothing almost as soon as created? Are such abilities made for no purpose? A brute arrives at a point of perfection which he can never pass. In a few years he has all the endowments he is capable of; and were he to live ten thousand more, would be the same thing he is at present. Were a human soul thus at a stand in her accomplishments, were her faculties to be full blown, and incapable of further enlargement, I could imagine it might fall away insensibly, and drop at once into a state of annihilation. But can we believe a thinking being, that is in a perpetual progress of improvement, and travelling on from perfection to perfection, after having just looked abroad into the works of the Creator, and made a few discoveries of his infinite goodness, wisdom, and power, must perish in her first setting out, and in the very beginning of her inquiries?"—*Spectator*, vol. ii.

What a lavish expenditure it would be, to give man such powers only to be cast down and annihilated! Suppose a man should construct, at great expense, a succession of machines, capable of accomplishing wonderful things, and then just as he had put them in operation, should dash them successively in pieces—what would be thought of him? Who would not stand amazed at his folly, and at the immense waste of time, materials, and property? Such folly and *waste* do those attribute to the Creator who deny man's immortal existence. If there is not a higher life for man, God really does more for the brute than the intelligent. Excluding violence, animals commonly live out their day, until they become incapable of more enjoyment. And then, too, they are free from those corroding anxieties, and fearful apprehensions which so often prey upon human minds. But man, after a life of anxiety and toil, is cut down in a moment, before he reaches the summit of desire, and before he accomplishes his wished-for end. Can it be that God does better for the beasts, than for man made in his image? Is it not a far more rational conclusion, drawn from all these facts, and in entire harmony with the dictates of infinite wisdom and love—that the soul of man is immortal?—that when his merely animal nature dies, and sinks to earth, his spirit will rise to a higher and more perfect sphere of being?

Such a destiny seems necessary to meet the demands of his nature, and to vindicate the wisdom and goodness of God in his creation.

ARGUMENT FROM INEQUALITIES IN PROVIDENCE.

The reality of a future life has been often and justly argued, from its necessity to vindicate the rectitude and benevolence of the Divine character and government in the unequal distribution of rewards and punishments in the present world.

Man comes into the world a helpless, and an imperfect being. He spends his infancy in obedience to his mere animal instincts, and his childhood and youth, for the most part, in folly and sin; and from the cradle, is not unfrequently doomed to uninterrupted disappointment, and bodily and mental suffering. "He is born to trouble as the sparks fly upward," and these come alike to the virtuous and the vicious. If God is just, and his government is founded in rectitude, and his providences are directed by equal and benevolent laws, we might reasonably suppose that men would prosper in life, and be exempt from trouble, affliction and sorrow, accordingly as they were righteous; and that, on the other hand, they would be rendered unprosperous, and suffer loss and sorrow in proportion to their sins. There can, in reality, be no even-handed justice—no impartial equity, where this great principle of government is not consistently and perfectly carried out.

But no such law, as a perfect, general, and undeviating rule, can be traced in the Divine administration in the present world. Though the vicious often suffer the consequences of their conduct, and the good often reap the peaceable fruits of virtue, yet we cannot turn and discern between the righteous and the wicked, from any developments of providence in their external prosperity, sufferings, or enjoyments. How often are the industrious and honest defeated in all their plans, and their hard-earned wages wrested from them, by dishonesty or misfortune, while the dishonest, and intriguing, and unprincipled are seemingly successful in all their plans and efforts, and prosper as the evergreen, whose leaf no chilling frost, or blasting wind, a wintry storm withers. How often are modesty and real worth overlooked, or put down by popular clamor; while the officious, the conceited, the proud and vicious are courted and exalted to places of trust, power and oppulence. How many virtuous and pious poor pine in solitude, and want, and neglect; while luxury, and sensuality, and prodigality revel amid princely grandeur and dishonest gain, in the mansions of the wicked. For how many long centuries have oppression and tyranny been suffered to hold their cruel and crushing sway over the liberties and rights of millions; turning into a blight the blessings, civil, temporal, and spiritual, which God designed to flow to man free and full as rivers of water.

These and other unnumbered inequalities in the administration of providence, have often exceedingly perplexed the minds of the wise and good in every age, and have sometimes led men to doubt or deny the existence of a superintending, directing God, in the affairs of men. Holy men of old felt, in their own experience, the full force of these perplexing difficulties. The Psalmist says, "But as for me, my feet were almost gone; my steps had well nigh slipped; when I saw the prosperity of the wicked," Ps. 73 : 2, 3. Jeremiah says, 12 : 1, "Righteous art thou, O Lord, when I plead with thee: let me talk with thee of thy judgments: wherefore doth the way of the wicked prosper? Wherefore are all they happy that deal very treacherously? Thou hast planted them, yea, they have taken root: they grow, yea, they bring forth fruit: thou art near in their mouth, and far from their reins." Habakkuk says, 1 : 13, "Thou art of purer eyes than to behold evil, and canst not look upon iniquity: wherefore lookest thou upon them that deal treacherously; and holdest thy tongue when the wicked devoureth the man that is more righteous than he?"

Now, who that leaves out of view a future life can solve these difficulties, in the government of a just and benevolent God? Who can show that there is rectitude, wisdom, or goodness in the Creator, if it is the whole of life to live only amid the inequalities, trials, and sufferings of the present world? The anxious mind says, there must be another life, if God is just and good—a life where all that is at present discordant and unequal shall be harmonized, and adjusted to principles of strictest equity. Such a life is essential to vindicate the character of God with men; and such a life as is revealed in Scripture will do it in perfection and beauty.

> "Ye vainly wise! ye blind presumptuous! Now,
> Confounded in the dust, adore that power,
> And wisdom oft arraign'd: see now the cause,
> Why unassuming worth in secret liv'd
> And died neglected: why the good man's share
> In life was gall and bitterness of soul:
> Why the lone widow and her orphans pin'd
> In starving solitude; while luxury,
> In palaces, lay straining her low thoughts,
> To form unreal wants: why heaven-born truth,
> And moderation fair, wore the red marks
> Of superstition's scourge: why licens'd pain,
> That cruel spoiler, that embosomed foe,
> Embitter'd all our bliss. Ye good distress'd!
> Ye noble few! who here unbending stand
> Beneath life's pressure, yet bear up awhile,
> And what your bounded view, which only saw
> A little part, deem'd evil is no more:
> Tho storms of wintry time will quickly pass,
> And one unbounded Spring encircle all"
>
> —THOMPSON.

DELIGHTFULLY ATTRACTIVE.

Viewed in this aspect, how delightful and attractive the prospects of a future world. It is only a little part of the plans and ways of God we can now see. They are only here developed in embryo, and we must see their end and reason before we can wisely judge of their rectitude, wisdom, and goodness. The government of God is a wheel within a wheel, vast, majestic, complicated, and eternal, and it will need an endless life to develop it to the comprehension and admiration of creatures. The voices of nature, everything within and around us, seem to suggest the idea of a future life. We feel that a fact upon which Scripture and reason so harmoniously blend, and shed their purest light, must be true. We accept it as a glorious hope, that man is immortal.

Amid the disappointments, the anxieties, the troubles, and sorrows of the present world, the attractions of a future life, as presented in the Word of God, are exceedingly great and joyous. When contrasted with the dark and cheerless prospect of the unbeliever, a belief in a future state addresses itself with longing desire, and delightful hope, to all the higher and purer principles of our nature. It is said that Beattie, the poet and philosopher, at one period of his life was involved in the darkness of scepticism; and that being afterwards converted to the enlivening, ennobling hope of another life, he wrote his Hermit, as descriptive of his own experience before and after his deliverance. Though familiar to every school-boy, its insertion may be the more welcome on this account, and serve better to illustrate the superior attractions of the world to come.

"At the close of the day, when the hamlet is still,
  And mortals the sweets of forgetfulness prove;
When naught but the torrent is heard on the hill,
  And naught but the nightingale's song in the grove.
'Twas thus by the cave of the mountain afar,
  While his harp rung symphonious, a hermit began,
No more with himself or with nature at war,
  He thought as a sage, though he felt as a man.

Ah! why all abandoned to darkness and woe;
  Why, lone Philomela, that languishing fall?
For spring shall return, and a lover bestow;
  And sorrow no longer thy bosom enthral.
But, if pity inspire thee, renew the sad lay—
  Mourn, sweetest complainer, man calls thee to mourn;
O, soothe him whose pleasures, like thine, pass away;
  Full quickly they pass—but they never return.

Now gliding remote, on the verge of the sky,
  The moon, half extinguished, her crescent displays;
But lately I mark'd, when majestic on high,
  She shone, and the planets were lost in her blaze.
Roll on then fair orb, and with gladness pursue
  The path that conducts thee to splendor again;
But man's faded glory, what change shall renew?
  Ah, fool! to exult in a glory so vain.

'Tis night, and the landscape is lovely no more;
  I mourn, but, ye woodlands, I mourn not for you;
For morn is approaching, your charms to restore,
  Perfumed with fresh fragrance, and glitt'ring with dew·
Nor yet for the ravage of winter I mourn;
  Kind nature, the embryo blossom will save;
But when shall spring visit the mould'ring urn?
  O, when shall day dawn on the night of the grave?

'Twas thus by the glare of false science betray'd
  That leads to bewilder; and dazzles to blind;
My thoughts went to roam from shade onward to shade,
  Destruction before me, and sorrow behind.

O, pity, great Father of light, then I cried,
  Thy creature, who fain would not wander from thee!
Lo, humbled in dust, I relinquish my pride;
  From doubt and from darkness thon only canst free.

And darkness and doubt are now flying away;
  No longer I roam in conjecture forlorn;
So breaks on the traveller, faint and astray,
  The bright and the balmy effulgence of morn.
See truth, love, and mercy, in triumph descending,
  And nature all glowing in Eden's first bloom!
On the cold cheek of death, smiles and roses are blending,
  And beauty immortal, awakes from the tomb."

Thus we see, that "In opposition to the desponding reflections and gloomy views of the sceptic, it inspires the virtuous mind with a lively hope, and throws a glorious radiance over the scenes of creation, and over every part of the government of the Almighty. It presents before us an unbounded scene, in which we may hope to contemplate the scheme of Providence in all its objects and bearings, where the glories of the divine perfections will be illustriously displayed, where the powers of the human mind will be perpetually expanding, and new objects of sublimity and beauty incessantly rising to view, in boundless perspective, worlds without end. It dispels the clouds which hang over the present and future destiny of man, and fully accounts for those longing looks into futurity which accompany us, at every turn, and those capacious powers of intellect, which cannot be fully exerted in the present life."—*Dick.*

This doctrine, then, gives an importance and a dignity to the existence and destiny of man, surpassingly grand and attractive. How vain a thing is human life, and how miserable a creature is man, if this life is the whole of his being! What really valuable end does he answer? What accomplish? All the noblest achievments of his intellect are nothing in fact, if life is extinguished at death. Virtue and vice then are empty names, and all that is called good or great in the world, is nothing elevated above the poorest reptile that creeps beneath his feet. But admitting man's future and endless life, what transcendant dignity and importance invest his existence even on earth?

Nothing could give more dignity, beauty, and consistency to human life than the prospects of an endless life beyond the grave. Let a man set this life to come before him as his great end, amid the trials and vicissitudes of time; let its bright hopes, and cheering prospects, animate him amid earth's sufferings and toils; and let him, having respect to the recompense of reward, cultivate that purity and rectitude of character in all things, which shall fit him most certainly for its enjoyment, and we could not conceive that he could pursue a more sublime and ennobling course. Can any object of earth be imagined equal to it, in glorious and attractive excellence? O ye vain grandeurs of courts! Ye sounding titles of kings, peers, nobles, senators, and presidents! Ye glittering and perishable wealth, so much coveted and adored! Ye gilded, vain and momentary pleasures of earth, what have ye to compare with the ennobling powers, and unfolding attractions of an immortal and endless life! What relief or consolation can ye give a dying mortal, when he is forced to descend into the dark valley whither ye cannot go; and where alone he must launch away into the unknown?

The great and the rich may have a splendid passage to the grave; they may die in state, and languish under a gilded canopy; they may expire on soft and downy pillows, and be respectfully attended by servants and physicians, and friends ready to render any aid or relief within the reach of human kindness or skill; but, oh! who of these will descend with them into the dark prison of the grave? And what real dignity can all this external wealth and pomp confer upon a loathsome corpse, which we cannot bear, and must bury from our sight? If the dead sleep in oblivion, and around all the future hang the dark and dismal clouds of gloomy annihilation, and man rises no more to higher scenes, what real attractions are there in all that earth calls good or great? What advantage then hath a man over the brute, or the insect, which flutters for its day in the sun-beams, and is no more? What real dignity, wealth, or beauty, attach to his being?

But suppose him now a candidate for an undying life, and that when he dies, there is a principle, living and immortal within, which rises, like the insect bursting forth from its chrysalis, to a more free and delightful sphere of being—and what beauty, glory, and nobleness, does it give to his existence even amid the imperfections of the present world.

How strange that any should wish to deny or disprove the soul's immortal destiny. Even supposing it a phantom, its delusion is infinitely more pleasing than the dreary prospects of the dark gulf of annihilation.

The bright hope which it inspires can sweeten every bitter cup of life, can soothe the asperities of affliction, render adversity joyous, and prompt man to purest and noblest deeds of virtue and goodness. Hence, then, ye profane! If the idea of another life is a delusion, let me alone amid its fancies. They are sweeter than the realities of life; they draw with cords more soft than silken; and possess attractions more strong than the central orb of light.

THERE IS HOPE FOR THE GUILTY.

It is true, that to the wicked, conscious of guilt, and fearful of judgment and retribution, a future life presents no attractions. But were such sure of a life of blessedness, how would the idea of immortality thrill the soul amid life's pilgrimage! How would it sweeten every bitter cup, and render joyous every trial and sorrow. But why may not all indulge this pleasing hope? Why not all look for glory and blessedness in a life to come? Does not mercy beckon in the gospel? and hope invite? and wisdom cry aloud,—"Let the wicked forsake his way, and the unrighteous man his thoughts; and let him return unto the Lord, and he will have mercy upon him; and to our God, for he will abundantly pardon?" *Is.* 55: 7. "As I live, saith the Lord God, I have no pleasure in the death of the wicked; but that the wicked turn from his way and live: turn ye, turn ye from your evil ways; for why will ye die?" *Ez.* 33: 11. "And the Spirit and the bride say come. And let him that heareth say come. And let him that is athirst come. And whosoever will let him take the water of life freely." *Rev.* 22: 17. "Ho, then, every one that thirsteth, come ye to the waters, and he that hath no money, come ye, buy and eat; yea, come buy wine and milk, without money and without price. *Is.* 55: 1. "Come now, and let us reason together, saith the Lord: though your sins be as scarlet, they shall be as white as snow; though they be red like crimson, they shall be as wool." *Is.* 1: 18. Why, then, will any die? Why need any despond? With such assurances of infinite love and mercy, why will not the wicked turn from his sins, and then look with undying joy and unbounded hope to heaven's pure and unending delights? If we would avoid the miserable consequences of sin *here*, we must forsake and turn from it, and so we must if we would escape its condemning power in an endless life. A mind conscious of impurity and crime cannot be happy here; it would not in heaven; it will not be in hell. There is no way, then, to avoid it but by repentance, and that faith in Jesus Christ which, in its practical results, purifies the heart, and fits for heaven.

O how should this hope of our immortal life inspire us with ceaseless desire and effort to escape sin, and every polluting principle and impure affection within us, and lead us day by day to seek that sanctifying grace which the gospel reveals, and that life of love, holiness, and obedience to God's commands, which, according to scripture and reason, give the only sure title to happiness.

CHAPTER III.

THE INTERMEDIATE STATE.

———— "The star that sets
Beyond the western wave, is not extinct;
It brightens in *another* hemisphere,
And gilds *another evening* with its rays.
O glorious hope of immortality!
At thought of thee, the coffin and the tomb
Affright no more, and e'en the monster Death,
Loses his fearful form, and seems a friend.
At thought of thee, my eager, glowing heart
Lets go its hold on sublunary bliss,
And longs to drop this cumbrous clog of earth,
And soar to bliss unfading and secure."

IT is not enough for us to know assuredly that there is another life to which man's spiritual nature shall rise, when the dissolution of his material shall remove him from the sphere of the living on earth. We need something more. We might know all this, and yet be in distressing doubt and gloomy suspense respecting the state of the soul in that separate and unseen world. To die then would indeed be taking a leap in the dark—would be launching away upon a dark and unknown ocean, with no sun, or star, or compass to guide.

> "To die;—to sleep;—
> To sleep? perchance to dream; aye, there's the rub;
> For in that sleep of death what dreams may come
> When we have shuffled off this mortal coil,
> Must give us pause!"

The uncertainty here intimated, respecting the condition of the soul in another life, is indeed distressing to every reflecting mind, and may well cause one to shrink back in—

> "Dread of something after death,—
> The undiscovered country, from whose bourne
> No traveller returns."

Hence we find that in every age numbers have resorted to fortune-tellers, astrologers, and magicians, not only, if possible, to discover the future events of life, but to unveil the unknown future world. And in our own day, how many eagerly run after the variously professed spiritual mediums to get some news from the spirit-land, and to learn something certainly respecting the state and condition of the departed. The desire thus manifested is natural, and it shows how anxious the human mind is to know the future.

Now, it is believed that the Scriptures not only reveal all that is necessary to regulate our conduct in reference to another life, and to sustain us under the trials and burdens of the present; but that they make known to us a scheme of future existence rational, consistent, beautiful and grand, and adapted to all the wants and aspirations of the mind, and to dissipate all uncertainty respecting the condition of the departed. These Scriptures constitute a more sure word of prophecy than all clairvoyant or mesmeric pretensions, "unto which ye do well that ye take heed, as unto a light that shineth in a dark place, until the day dawn, and the day-star arise in your hearts."—2 *Peter*, 1: 19. And well would it have been for the world had men been content to follow this "sure word," instead of those *ignes fatui* which float amid the marshes and bogs of honest, it may be, but disturbed imaginations.

A COMMON ERROR.

Various errors and vain conceits respecting the condition and destiny of man in the world to come have gained currency among professed Christians, from inattention to the revelations of heaven as a whole, or from seeking to reduce the teachings of Scripture to a pre-conceived theory, and mingling with them the deductions of their own philosophy.

One prominent error which prevails, and which is very commonly taught, is, that the departed, immediately after death, *are judged*, and enter at once upon their glorious and eternal reward. If the reader has been taught thus to believe, let him not be startled, when we affirm, that this view of the future is most clearly contradicted in Scripture. The great and peculiar reward of the righteous, as well as the sentence of the wicked, are not at, or immediately after death, but at the second coming of our Lord--the resurrection of the dead, and the final judgment. So commonly and frequently is this presented in Scripture as a great and important fact, that it is surprising that it should ever have been overlooked. Let the following Scriptures be diligently pondered :—

Luke, 14 : 13–14, "But when thou makest a feast, call the poor, the maimed, the lame, the blind ; and thou shalt be blessed : for they cannot recompense thee ; for thou shalt be recompensed *at the resurrection of the just.*" There is no allusion here to death, as the time at which they are to be rewarded ; but overlooking all intermediate states, or events, our Lord refers the just directly and only to the *resurrection*, as the time when they should be recompensed for all their charities and labors of love.

Luke, 20 : 34–36, "And Jesus answering, said unto them, The children of this world marry, and are given in marriage : but they which shall be counted worthy to obtain that world, and the *resurrection* of the dead, neither marry, nor are given in marriage : neither can they die any more : for they are equal unto the angels ; and are the children of God, being the children of the *resurrection.*" In this passage, also, it is seen that the great and peculiar rewards of the righteous are associated only with the resurrection ; and if this is true, their reward cannot be at death.

Acts, 24 : 15, "And have hope toward God, which they themselves also allow, that there shall be a resurrection of the dead, both of the just and unjust." This shows that the hope of the apostle, respecting future blessedness, was intimately associated with the resurrection. See, also, *Acts*, 26 : 6.

2 *Tim.* 4 : 6–8, "For I am now ready to be offered, and the time of my departure is at hand. I have fought a good fight, I have finished my course, I have kept the faith: henceforth there is laid up for me a crown of righteousness, which the Lord, the righteous Judge, shall give me *at that day*, and not to me only, but unto all them, also, who love *his appearing*." It is clear from this, that the apostle did not expect his crown until the resurrection-day —the day of Christ's glorious appearing. And if his expectation was according to truth, then he has not yet received the crown for which he contended; but is even now waiting in some state of happy and glorious expectancy. The same is taught in Titus, 2 : 11–14.

1 *Peter*, 1 : 3–7, "Blessed be the God and Father of our Lord Jesus Christ, which, according to his abundant mercy, has begotten us again unto a lively hope, by the resurrection of Jesus Christ from the dead, to an inheritance incorruptible and undefiled, and that fadeth not away, *reserved in heaven* for us, who are kept by the power of God, through faith unto salvation, *ready to be revealed in the last time*." And this *last time* is explained in verse seventh, to denote *the* appearing of Jesus Christ. Death is not alluded to here; but beyond this the eye of the believer is directed to the second personal appearing

of Christ, as the time when the inheritance reserved in heaven for them will be bestowed.

John, 5 : 28, 29, "Marvel not at this: for the hour is coming, in the which all that are in their graves shall hear his voice, and shall come forth; they that have done good, unto the resurrection of life; and they that have done evil, unto the resurrection of condemnation." How clearly are the life and death, threatened in Scripture, associated in this passage with the resurrection. What our Lord says in *Matt.* 10 : 15, 11 : 24, of Sodom and Gomorrah, in in the day of judgment, shows that they are reserved unto the judgment day for the decision in their case. The inhabitants of these ancient cities, as well as those of Tyre and Sidon, who had perished from earth long before the advent of our Saviour, it is said, will receive their peculiar condemnation at that great day which God has appointed, in which he will judge the world in righteousness by that man whom he hath ordained, whereof he hath given assurance unto all men in that he hath raised him from the dead. But why this, if they were judged and rewarded at death? Where, in a single passage, is it said that any are judged at death?

The doctrine advocated is still more clearly set forth in 2 *Pet.* 2 : 9, and 3 : 7, "The Lord knoweth how to deliver the godly out of temptations, and *to reserve the unjust unto the day of judgment* to be punished. But the heavens and the earth, which are now, by the same word *are kept in store*, reserved unto fire against the day of judgment, and perdition of ungodly men." These passages need no comment. They teach that none of the unjust who have died, have yet received their sentence and doom. They are reserved, in the place appointed for them, until the judgment-day arrives. They probably know that they will be condemned, from the place in which they are confined, and from the fearful looking for of judgment which torments them in their prison-house, but their trial has not yet been held, nor their sentence pronounced. They are like criminals arrested and confined in prison, awaiting the day of trial.

Neither are the fallen angels yet judged and punished. *Peter* says, "God spared not the angels that sinned, but cast them down to hell, and delivered them into chains of darkness, *to be reserved unto judgment.*" 2 *Pet.* 2 : 4. *Jude* says, "And the angels which kept not their first estate, but left their own habitation, he hath *reserved* in everlasting chains under darkness *unto the judgment of the great day.*" The expression, everlasting chains under darkness, is doubtless a figure, drawn from the manner of securing prisoners, and is employed to represent the entire security in which these fallen beings are reserved in the places appointed. No language could declare more clearly that the devils are not yet judged and punished. And with this accords the address of the demons to our Lord, *Matt.* 8 : 29, "And behold, they cried out, saying, What have we to do with thee, Jesus, thou Son of God? Art thou come hither to torment us *before the time?*" The time then appointed for their torment had not yet come in the days of our Lord, though they had fallen thousands of years before; and as the day of Judgment has not yet come, they are still in the same condition in which they were, in respect to punishments as in former times.

In *Romans*, 2 : 7, 16, The Apostle declares that God will render to every man according to his works, *in the day in which* he will judge the secrets of all men according to the Gospel. And this manifestly affirms that no one will be rewarded according to his works until the final day of judgment.

The parable of the sheep and goats, *Matt.* 25 . 31–34, teaches that the righteous will not be put in possession of the kingdom prepared for them from the foundation of the world, nor the wicked sentenced, until the Son of Man comes in his glory, and all his holy angels with him. These various scriptures now noticed, fully confirm the position taken, that the inheritance and rewards promised, are not entered upon at death, but are reserved, or laid up, against the last time, to be manifested and bestowed at the resurrection and judgment. We cannot call to mind a passage, in which the doctrine is taught, that judgment and reward take place at death. The parable of the rich man and Lazarus does not prove it. Nothing is said in this of any trial or judgment passed upon them, or any reward formally bestowed. The comfort or repose of Lazarus, and the misery of Dives are all that are affirmed, just as a good man might be said to be happy, and a bad man miserable in the present state.

A NECESSARY DISTINCTION.

It has often been affirmed, and may still appear to some, that all this is a matter of no practical importance, as the destiny of every individual is in fact decided, by the relation he has sustained to God, and the character he has formed in the present world, so that no change will, or can be, effected in the allotments beyond the grave.

It is granted to be a clearly-revealed scriptural truth, that the character formed here, and the works done, will fix the destiny of men hereafter; but the aspects in which the Scriptures present this subject, are vastly more important to the consistency and harmony of Divine truth, and to the revealed order and developments of the life to come, than might at first view appear.

The doctrines of the resurrection of the dead, and of a judgment day to come, are manifestly great and fundamental truths of Scripture, and cannot be denied without an abandonment of much that is most impressive and effective in the Gospel. But what need is there of a resurrection of our bodies, and of a day of judgment, if men are judged at death, and enter upon the full rewards of the world to come, independently of their resurrection bodies? The practical tendency of this unscriptural view, is to lessen in human estimation the importance or necessity of a future resurrection and judgment; and thus to divert the mind from those great points in our future destiny, which God has so affectingly and prominently presented. And this is one reason, we doubt not, why those doctrines are so often disregarded and denied, at the present day, among professing Christians. For how natural and logical the inference—that if the soul is now imprisoned in the body, and can best attain the glorious destiny in reserve, as is often asserted in popular writings, in its disembodied state; and if men are accordingly judged and rewarded immediately after death—there is no necessity for a resurrection and judgment. If the soul, freed from this cumbrous body, is at death in a more favorable situation for progress and happiness, and does in fact enter upon the full destiny in reserve—then these doctrines, as they have been commonly understood, cannot be true. It is only in some spiritual or mystic sense that they are to be understood. Thus, the direct tendency of prevalent views upon this subject, among orthodox Christians, is to error and scepticism on these all-glorious and fundamental points.

The proper and Scriptural aspects of these doctrines will be considered in their appropriate place; but it may be important here to remark that, according to Scripture, man's highest destiny is to be attained in connection with his body, and that there is a most manifest propriety, wisdom and justice, in the arrangement by which men are referred to the future great day of judgment for the decision in their case, and their eternal reward.

God has declared it to be the great principle of

his government to render to every man according to his works. The righteous will be judged and rewarded according to their works wrought in Christ Jesus, and the wicked according to their deeds done in selfishness and sin. Hence, it is rendered, we conceive, absolutely necessary that the reward of all should be deferred until the judgment day; because, before that time, it cannot be known to created beings how much good or evil any have done. The character and desert of our deeds are to be determined by the motives from which they spring, and by the influence for good or evil which they exert. The influence of a man's life and deeds constitute, in fact, the greater part of what he does in life. His simple and naked acts, separated from all their influence and their consequences on unborn generations, are not the chief things to be taken into the account in forming that estimate of his deeds, according to which he is to be rewarded. The influence he exerts is the most important. This does not die. After a man is dead, it travels on in its consequences of good or evil to the end. Many do vastly more good, and others immensely more evil after death, than while living. The prophets who wrote the Old Testament, and the evangelists and apostles who wrote the New, have exerted a wider influence for good since their death than while living. All along down the track of ages, and at the present time, they have been, and are doing, untold good. And so every one who writes. Baxter, though dead, yet speaketh. So does Paine.

The blighting influence of his Age of Reason travels on, widening as a stream of death in its dark course, and none of these can be justly rewarded according to their works, until the close of that dispensation which is to circumscribe their peculiar operations on earth.

If good men then, and holy, are to be rewarded according to their works, they will not be prepared to receive their recompense until their good is accomplished in the present time. And so with the wicked, we cannot see how justice can be fully awarded, or their doom appreciated, until the mischief they have wrought shall find its limit in the closing up of the present dispensation.

For this reason we can see that there is wisdom and necessity, in referring all men to the great day of judgment, for the final decision in their case. And then again, as one great object of the judgment day is to vindicate the ways of God with men before the universe, and to make such a demonstration of the equity and rectitude of the Divine government, that all the good shall approve and admire the ways of God; it will be far more impressive and grand in the result, to have the judgment, in each individual case, rendered at the same time, or in the same connection, than it would be to assign men their destiny at death, under circumstances where all could not see or appreciate the result, and before the good or evil of their doings were developed.

As God foreknows from the beginning the manifold results of all actions, he might judge and assign each one his reward of honor or dishonor at death; but then the moral effect, upon interested worlds, would seemingly be lost, and we could not judge of the righteousness of his proceedings. We doubt not that there will be seen to be an infinite wisdom in postponing the reward of the righteous and of the wicked until the resurrection and judgment of the great day.

Assuming, for the present, the truth of the resurrection of the dead at some future period, and of a great and final day of account, then it is manifest that between death, and the resurrection and judgment, there is an *intermediate state*—a state differing vastly, in many particulars, from the present embodied state in the flesh; and as widely different, as we can well conceive, from that higher and more glorious resurrection state which will succeed, and when the peculiar rewards of righteousness and unrighteousness will be conferred.

The doctrine of a resurrection, when these vile bodies of ours shall be changed, and fashioned like unto Christ's glorious body, necessarily implies an intermediate state, clearly defined, in which the soul is not advanced to that state of promised and renowned blessedness, in which, in an embodied form, it will pursue its upward career during the unending ages which will follow.

Now, it is an interesting inquiry, where is the soul, during this interval? What is its state and condition? Its prospects and enjoyments? Do the

Scriptures shed any definite light on the subject? If they do, it is our duty and privilege, to listen and learn all that God has been pleased to communicate.

CONSCIOUS EXISTENCE.

1. The souls of the departed *are, during the intermediate state, in a conscious existence.* It has been maintained by some, "that the period which elapses between the time of death and the resurrection, is spent in unconsciousness and in inactivity; that the soul is either extinct, or in a profound and dreamless sleep, forgetful of all that is past, ignorant of all that is around it, and regardless of all that is to come." This opinion has been greatly revived in these latter times, by those who hold that natural death is the peculiar penalty of sin, and that eternal life, by the resurrection of the good to immortality, is the peculiar gift of Jesus Christ. But this theory seems to be plainly contradicted by the Word of God. The Saviour said to the penitent thief on the cross, "To-day shalt thou be with me in paradise." The rich man and Lazarus are both represented in the parable, by our Lord, as alive, and conscious, and capable of thinking, feeling and speaking. Moses and Elias, departed saints, are said to have appeared unto Jesus and his three disciples, on the Mount of Transfiguration, and to have conversed with them.—*Matt.* 17 : 3. Moses, therefore, as well as Elias in his transfigured body, must have been

alive and conscious. And if Moses, why not all others?

When the apostle John was about to worship the angel, sent to him in Patmos, to communicate the message of Jesus, He said, "See thou do it not: for I am thy fellow-servant, *and of thy brethren the prophets*, and of them which keep the sayings of this book: worship God.—*Rev.* 22 : 9.

Our Lord, in his argument with the Sadducees, who denied the existence of angels and spirits, said, Matt. 22 : 31, 32, "But as touching the resurrection of the dead, have ye not read that which was spoken unto you by God, saying, I am the God of Abraham, and the God of Isaac, and the God of Jacob? *God is not the God of the dead, but of the living.*" The language here is peculiar. Jehovah says, *I am*, and not I shall be, in some future age, the God of these patriarchs. And as Christ affirms that God is not the God of the dead—of that which does not exist, but of the living, it proves that Abraham, Isaac, and Jacob, though dead and buried, in respect to their bodies, were living beings at the time our Lord spoke; and therefore confirms the separate and conscious existence of souls after death.

The prayer of Stephen, *Acts* 7 : 59, immediately before his death, shows that he believed in the existence of the soul separate from the body. "And they stoned Stephen, calling upon God, and saying, Lord Jesus, receive my spirit." So the wise man tells us, "Then," at death, "shall the dust return to the earth as it was: and the spirit shall return unto God who gave it." There are various other scriptures which assert, even more strongly than these, the separate existence of the soul, after the body returns to earth, but which are here omitted, because they can be more conveniently introduced in another place. It would seem then that the teachings of the Word of God are as full and explicit on the great doctrine of the soul's immortality as could be desired.

——— "The star that sets
Beyond the western wave, is not extinct;
It brightens in *another* hemisphere,
And gilds *another evening* with its rays."

THE RIGHTEOUS WITH CHRIST.

2. The souls of believers go at death to heaven, and are with Christ during the intermediate state; while the souls of the wicked go to their own place, and are kept in reserve until the resurrection and judgment. In the Roman Catholic, and in the Episcopal churches, not only an intermediate state, but an intermediate *place* is maintained. Thus the Rector of Trinity Church, Wilmington, Delaware, writes, "The great majority of those who die in the Lord, are very far from being eminent saints. They leave the world pardoned and free from sin, indeed, but very imperfect, ignorant, feeble, and unfit for the ineffable blaze of heavenly effulgence, and the society and employments of the ancient and glorious inhabitants of heaven. But Paradise *is an interme-*

diate resting-place, where the soul becomes unfolded, invigorated, and instructed for a superior state and world.

"The spirit, disenthralled and emancipated from its earthly prison and vehicle, passes into this *place* of abode, perfectly adapted to its disembodied state, and the design of that state. There under genial and sensitive influences, it repairs its losses and injuries, recovers its balance and tone, becomes thoroughly developed, and fully prepared for another and still higher state of being."

According to this, Paradise, or the intermediate abode of the departed, is not the purgatory of the catholic church, but a kind of school preparatory to the higher glories of the resurrection state.

But this theory of an intermediate place somewhere beneath, or this side of heaven, seems to be clearly contradicted by express Scripture testimony. Let it be remembered that it is repeatedly declared, that when our Lord ascended on high, he went into heaven itself, where he ever liveth. The apostle says, Heb. 8 : 1, "Now of the things which we have spoken, this is the sum: we have such an high priest who is set on the right hand of the throne of the Majesty in the heavens." And again, 9 : 24, "For Christ is not entered into the holy place made with hands, which are the figures of the true; but into *heaven itself*, ever to appear in the presence of God for us."

It is then a clearly revealed truth that the Saviour has ascended into heaven itself, and no intermediate place, as we can perceive, in the revelations of a future world.

But where Christ is, *there,* we are assured, his saints are, and as it is certain that he is in heaven, they must also be there. "Father," he prays, "I will that those whom thou hast given me, *be* with me, that they may behold my glory." In accordance with this, Stephen, when about to die, cried, "Lord Jesus, receive my spirit." The apostle Paul says of himself and all whom he represented, 2 *Cor.* 5 : 6, "Therefore we are always confident, knowing that, whilst we are at home in the body, we are absent from the Lord: we are confident, I say, and willing rather to be absent from the body, *and to be present with the Lord.*" It would seem from this, that the apostle *confidently* expected that when believers should be separated from the body at death, they would from that time be ever present with the Lord, which not only shows his belief in the separate existence of the soul, but also that he thought not of an intermediate place.

The same thing is expressed in *Phil.* 1 : 23, "For I am in a strait betwixt two, having a desire to depart and be with Christ, which is far better." Is it not clear from this that he expected, when he departed this life, to be immediately present with Christ in heaven itself? On any other supposition, his desire to depart, that he might be with Christ, would be unintelligible. For if saints go not immediately to heaven, where Christ is, but to some intermediate place, then by dying he would have been no sooner with the Lord, than he would by remaining on earth, nor so near as to enjoyment; for here he had access to him by prayer and endeared spiritual intercourse

In harmony with these confident and ardent expectations of the apostle, he teaches, in 1 *Thess.* 4 : 14, that at the second coming of Christ, all the saints who have died will come with him. "For if we believe that Jesus died and rose again, even so them also which sleep in Jesus, will God bring with him." Is it not clearly implied here, that all the saints are with Christ, and hence will come with him, when he descends to earth at the resurrection and judgment? We embrace it, then, as a most joyous and consoling truth, that death ushers the believer into the presence of Christ, there to remain in happy and glorious expectancy, waiting for the edemption of the body. But this being with Christ, simply, is not the great and peculiar reward promised. Our redemption and likeness to him are tc be complete. Our vile bodies are to be changed, and fashioned like unto his glorified body—and then we are to be unto him kings and priests, to sit down with him on his throne, and to share with him the glories of his everlasting kingdom—all of which will be more fully discussed in the chapter on the *nature* of future happiness. None of these honors will, according to Scripture, be conferred until the resurrection.

THE FORM OF THE SOUL.

3. The soul, we believe, enters the world of spirits, and exists during the intermediate state, in its appropriate human form. To every reflecting mind the question will sometimes arise, what is the *form* of the soul, and in what shape does it exist when it is disembodied? Upon this subject many vain and irrational conceits have been entertained. But the most simple, natural, rational, and scriptural idea is, that the soul has a human form—a form corresponding to the body, and that it therefore enters and exists in the spirit world in its own distinctive form, so that the departed may not only recognize themselves, but every other being with whom on earth they have been acquainted.

This idea is prominent in the system of Swedenborg; but with him it was not original. It is the simple and only idea of the Bible in the literal sense. It is not a subject treated of directly, or taught in definite propositions—but everywhere in Scripture, when the departed are spoken of, or when they are represented as making their appearance to others, they are always in their appropriate human form. Abraham and Lazarus were so seen by Dives, and Dives by them. Moses and Elias appeared as men, and the great multitude which John saw in vision around the throne, were as human beings, in their appropriate form. And hence when Christians speak of meeting, or seeing their loved ones in another life, they have, in general, no other idea of them, than in the very forms in which they were on earth. And so Virgil and other ancients, in describing those seen in the infernal and celestial regions, represent them all.

This is certainly a very natural and rational idea, so much so that it is not at all surprising that it should everywhere be assumed in Scripture as an undoubted truth, without exposition, note, or comment. As the Scriptures, then, uniformly represent the departed in human forms, we are certainly justified in the conclusion that such is indeed the form of those who have entered the spirit world.

Nor is it true that this is unworthy of notice, or unimportant. We love to take the Bible as it reads, and to receive the simple impress of its communicated truth, unperverted by metaphysical inductions, which have no foundation in nature or common sense. To be permitted to look into the spirit world, through the simple medium of Scripture, and contemplate the departed as they gather round the Saviour, as human beings, is adapted to give a more definite conception of another life, and more pleasing, than to think of spirits as some intangible gauzy existences, flitting about in empty air, without figure.

The attractions of the world to come, and its power over us, will doubtless be strong in proportion to the clearness of our views of its wondrous realities. How can we be strongly attracted by anything which we do not clearly perceive or definitely comprehend? Any view, therefore, authorized by the Word of God, which is adapted to give more clear and pleasing conceptions of another life, must increase its attractive influence.

LONGINGS OF NATURE.

It would detract exceedingly from the pleasurable anticipations of meeting departed friends in another life, did we know that they were not still in their identified human forms. To indulge the sentiment is natural and innocent. The desire is enshrined in our common humanity. Even the mother, whose smiling infant is taken from her arms, longs to meet and embrace it just as it was, in its infantile form. If any tell her that "not as a child," shall she again behold it, her language is,—

"O say not so! how shall I know my darling,
If changed her form, and veil'd with shining hair,
If, since her flight, has grown my starling,
How shall I know her there?
On memory's page, by viewless fingers painted,
I see the features of my angel child;
She passed away ere vice her life had tainted,
Passed to the undefiled.

"O say not so! for I could clasp her, even
As when below she lay upon my breast
I would dream of her as a bud in heaven,
Amid the blossoms blest.
My little one, she was a folded lily,
Sweeter than any on the azure wave,
But night came down, a starless night and chilly
Alas! we could not save.

Yes, as a child, serene and noble poet—
O heaven were dark were children wanting there,

I hope to clasp my bud, as when I wore it,
A dimpled baby fair.
Though years have flown, toward my blue-eyed daughter,
My heart yearns ofttimes with a mother's love;
Its never-dying tendrils now enfold her,
E'en as a child above.

E'en as a babe, my little dove-eyed daughter,
Nestle and coo upon my heart again :
Wait for thy mother by the river water,
It shall not be in vain.
Wait as a child,—how shall I know my darling,
If changed her form, and veiled with shining hair ;
If, since her flight, has grown my little starling,
How shall I know her there ?"

The tender sentiment here breathed is very common, more so than many would imagine. But the mother may never meet her babe just as it was. Will its powers not expand and thus its aspects vary? No parent on reflection, would wish to have her child remain eternally in a state of infancy. Reason shows that it would be vastly more pleasing to meet them in some enlarged and advanced sphere of being. The demands of our yearning natures are fully met if we may think of them still as retaining their human form, though progressing—if we may trace in their glorified and developed forms the family likeness and lineaments inscribed on earth.

THE CHARACTER OF THE SOUL.

The Scriptures clearly teach that we shall enter the spirit world sustaining essentially the same moral character which we cultivated in life, and possessed when we left the world.

Perhaps when we cross the river of death we shall be surprised to find that we are so much like ourselves, and so much under the influence of the same affections which controlled us on earth. For there is no ground from Scripture or reason to suppose that the soul changes its nature, essence, or character in passing from one world to another. "Death, like birth, is the act of passing from one state of existence to another, giving us nothing but a change of situation. Here are two moments of time. Now there is the spirit of a man still tremblingly dwelling within an expiring body. Next moment, the same spirit lives without the body. The little words, *in* and *out*, contain the only difference. All that the soul is at death, it *will be* after death; nothing less, nothing more. It varies nothing. It leaves nothing of itself. It only goes." Why then must we not possess the same moral character in the spirit, as in the present world?

The Scriptures teach that "the wicked shall be driven away in his wickedness; and it is certainly the common belief, that *they* will enter and continue to exist in another life, cherishing the same enmity to God, and possessing the same worldly character in other respects which they cultivated on earth.

The following passage teaches that what is true of the wicked will be of the righteous. *Rev.* 22 : 11.—"And he saith unto me, Seal not the sayings of the prophecy of this book: for the time is at hand. He that is unjust, let him be unjust still: and he which is filthy, let him be filthy still: and he which is righteous, let him be righteous still: and he that is holy, let him be holy still."

The doctrine of this passage seems plainly to be, that as men die, so they will enter another life. The present is one of preparation, and it is here that our characters are to be decided. And yet, in respect to the righteous especially, there must, and doubtless will be, great changes pass upon them for the better. Even the best will enter the future world encompassed with imperfections, ignorance and error. And it will be necessary that they shall be delivered from all moral imperfection and error to prepare them for the fruits and rewards of holiness, in the presence and enjoyment of God.

And we can see, that there will be an entire adaptation, in the altered circumstances produced by a change of worlds, to produce the desired result. The period of probation, and the season of trial and conflict will then be forever passed; and the day of perfect victory and joyful triumph will have dawned in beauty upon the Spirit. This altered condition in the circumstances of their being will produce changes of vital import. They will no longer live amid scenes of sin, or breathe an atmosphere infected with evil. There will hence be no enticements to evil, or incentives to disobedience. There will be no longer any danger of contamination or seduction, from a necessary association with the impure; for, the society of earth, will at death be exchanged for the society of Jesus—of angels, and the spirits of the just made perfect. There will no longer be any danger of mistake in the reception of truth, or delusion from a darkened mind; for, amid the society of the just, the sun of righteousness and the gleamings of truth, pure from the fountain of light, will henceforth dissipate the mists of error, and chase away forever the darkness of untruth.

Now in such circumstances, and under such genial influences, we may well suppose, that souls which have been redeemed and regenerated on earth, and to whose upward aspirings a real impulse has been given by the breath and power of the eternal Spirit—will rapidly develop their moral powers to perfection—burst away from the shackles of ignorance and sin, and clothe themselves in the white robes of unspotted purity.

Take the rose, which in some secluded and unfavorable spot has begun to put forth its tender leaves, and whose bud has begun to swell under some genial warmth which it has received, and bring it out to the pure light, and balmy air, and warming influences of the sun, and how soon it will expand, and burst forth in beauty, and exhale its sweetness on the air.

So minds, in which the principle of holiness has been implanted on earth, and which has begun to germinate and bud, even amid the untoward influences of time, we may well suppose, will soon burst forth in perfection and beauty, when placed amid and beneath the pure light, warmth and influence of heaven.

But let it be observed, that all this will not be an essential change of character, but only an enlargement and development of that already formed in all its essential ingredients. The rose could not be developed, were there not previously life in its roots and stock, and a bud upon its branch. The child unborn is a man in miniature, and undergoes no change in nature, or the essential elements of its being when born into the world. He is only introduced to a new life—to a new sphere of being, and is placed in circumstances more favorable for the ultimate development of his powers. So in passing out of the body into another sphere of life we shall assume no new characters. We shall be just like ourselves. There will only be, in the processes of another life, a development of characters already formed, like the buds ready to burst in the spring. The unholy will be unholy still, and the righteous will be righteous still.

How long a time will be required to free the souls of the regenerated from all the errors which have been incorporated into the habits of their minds and modes of thought, and from every taint of moral defilement which has left its stain upon them, we are not informed, and it is not essential for us to know. Were it revealed, that during this intermediate state, the mind under the genial, sanative and spiritual influences which have been described, would gradually, and according to the natural and voluntary operations of the laws of mind, "repair its losses and injuries," and thus, according to the same laws of sanctification which now exist, and in connection with the exercise of its own powers, become thoroughly prepared for another and still higher state of being at the resurrection, it would not seem unreasonable. It may be so. Such a supposition is more in accordance with the laws of the human mind, and more in harmony with all that we know of the method of God's working, than the idea that all our sins and imperfections are to be stricken out in an unconscious instant of time at death by some miraculous energy, and without any effort of our own to attain the end. We know of nothing contrary to this view in the written Word. But as it is a point not revealed, we are not presumptuously to inquire respecting it.

One point is clearly settled. The great and essential elements of our future characters must be gathered this side of the grave. Here the true and tried corner-stone must be laid, upon which the eternal structure of perfection and blessedness must be reared; for there can be no radical change effected hereafter. It is to be feared that multitudes in the church and out of it fatally mistake here, and depend more upon the change to be wrought in them *at* or *after death* to fit them for heavenly happiness, than upon their earnest efforts *now* to become holy, and to bring every thought, and feeling, and purpose into subjection to the law of Jesus Christ. But surely any such hope is presumptuous and unscriptural. There is no promise of holiness or happiness in heaven to any who do not now "hunger and thirst after righteousness," and who do not "follow after holiness, without which no man shall see the Lord."

O how often have I trembled at the grave of many a departed professor, when I have known how little of the loveliness, the meekness, patience and humility of the Gospel they manifested—how vain, foolish, and inconsistent were their lives, and how feeble were their efforts, if any were made, to grow in grace and in the knowledge of our Lord and Saviour Jesus Christ. I know that God is infinitely benevolent—that his compassions vastly transcend the purest exhibitions of human love; but will he reward the unfaithful servant? Has he promised to fill any with holiness and happiness who do not hunger and thirst after righteousness. It is written that to those only, who by a faithful continuance in well-doing, seek for glory, honor, and immortality, will he render eternal life.—*Rom.* 2. Justification, through the abounding mercy of God in Christ, gives a title to heaven; but it is never bestowed except in connection with that regeneration and sanctification which consecrates the heart and life to the high and holy pursuits of the world to come, by a cordial submission and obedience to the will of God.

Do not those strangely deceive themselves, who live conformed to a wicked world—who can do things that even the unrenewed condemn, and who labor not to cultivate the graces of the Spirit, and yet suppose that God, by some divine ictus, or electric shock, will strike out all their sins, in an unconscious instant, between the last pulsations of life and their sudden entrance into the spirit world? What evidence can we have that we are justified and regenerated, except as the spirit of holiness reigns within us, and leads us to live in obedience to the pure and virtuous and benevolent principles of the gospel?

THE REPOSE OF THE SOUL.

5. The souls of the righteous, during the intermediate state, will exist rather in a condition of rest or repose, than of activity. This is affirmed in various scriptures.

Rev. 14 : 13. "And I heard a voice from heaven, saying unto me, write, Blessed are the dead which die in the Lord from henceforth: yea, saith the spirit, *that they may rest* from their labors; and their works do follow them." This directly affirms a state of rest—of tranquil, peaceful, and joyous repose, rather than an active state of diligent pursuit. *Rev.* 6 : 10, 16, "And they cried with a loud voice, saying, How long, O Lord, holy and true, dost thou not judge and avenge our blood on them that dwell on the earth? And white robes were given unto every one of them, and it was said unto them *that they should rest yet for a little season*, until their fellow-servants also and their brethren, that should be killed as they were, should be fulfilled." Does not this passage represent the martyrs, and by inference all the dead, as existing in the world of spirits, in a condition of *holy rest* and *expectancy*, which will continue until the whole company of the redeemed, up to the end of the dispensation, shall be gathered in, when in company and together they shall be introduced to their glorious reward? In accordance with these passages—we are assured, *Heb.* 4 : 9, that, There *remaineth a rest* for the people of God.

The same idea of a soothing and peaceful rest in reserve for the righteous after death, is presented in those scriptures which represent the good when dying, as falling asleep—asleep in Jesus. Of Stephen it is said, when he died, *he fell asleep.* This is a common expression to represent the death of the just. Of all the righteous departed, the apostle says, "For if we believe that Jesus died and rose again, even so them also which *sleep in Jesus* will God bring with him." 1 Thess. 4 : 14. Now were any disposed to press this figure to its utmost limit, and to maintain a strict and literal analogy, in all respects, between the sleeping, and the dead in Christ; an unconscious state could not here be inferred; for, in our sleep "what dreams do come!" How many that are exceedingly pleasant and enrapturing, exceeding even the gayest and most joyous day-dreams which ever crossed the imagination. And were our intermediate state to be strictly analogous to that of sleep, the expression, "*asleep in Jesus*," would give us an assurance that no fearful, distressing, or troubled dreams would disturb our slumbers; but would rather lead us to expect that all our slumbering visions of future reward and blessedness would be of the most peaceful and pleasurable kind.

But the idea which the Holy Ghost designed to convey under the image of "balmy sleep" is, we judge, that of sweet and delightful repose, a rest from all the trials, sorrows, anxieties, toils, and wearisome labors of life. And what figure could more appropriately and attractively represent that repose, for which the good, tempest-tost, and afflicted, now often sigh, than to sleep in Jesus? It is a delightful image of the future, to the afflicted people of God. Job, in the midst of his severe trials, longed for rest in the grave, or invisible world, 3 : 17; and the Psalmist sighed for some peaceful refuge, far removed beyond the stormy afflictions of the world. "And I said, oh, that I had wings like a dove; for then would I fly away and be at rest. Lo, then I would wander far off, and remain in the wilderness. I would hasten my escape from the windy storm and tempest." And so there remaineth a rest for the people of God, prior to those higher activities, which will be entered upon in the resurrection state.

These Scriptures show conclusively that during the intermediate state, the righteous will be rather in a state of rest than activity—not rest, in the sense of unconsciousness or idleness, but rest in respect to those offices they are afterwards to fill, and those high services they are to perform in the kingdom of God, in the resurrection state.

In the resurrection, the dead in Christ will no longer sleep in Jesus, but will awake to a new and an immortal life, in association with their material bodies, and to activities and progressions, of which we can now form no conception.

We regard the Scriptures, above quoted, as having reference to the condition of the soul during the intermediate state, and not as intended to characterize the whole career of an endless life. It seems to us that this view is essential, to give consistency and harmony to the representations of revelation, respecting the high destinies of the eternal world.

ITS RECEPTIVE STATE.

It would be in harmony with these Scriptures to regard the soul as existing, during the intermediate state, in a passive, receptive condition. It may be analogous to that of infancy and childhood. During the first years of a child's existence on earth, its mind is passively receptive of those impressions and ideas, which are designed to prepare it for the higher duties and responsibilities of manhood. Its mind may be said to be at rest during the first months of its life, and in such a state as to be continually receiving those impressions which are to expand and bring into active exercise, at the appropriate time, its own latent and inherent powers.

Such may be the state of the soul during the years which shall precede the resurrection morn; and this may be the intent of the rest that remains. It cannot be doubted that the mind will receive wonderful impressions and ideas, as it enters the heavenly world, and holds converse with Jesus and the glorified. And these impressions of heaven's own image and spirit will be continually increasing, and they must necessarily expand and purify the soul beyond all present conception. And can it be questioned that these impressions and ideas, thus received, will prepare the saved for the higher services of unending ages? It seems reasonable, therefore, to regard the rest that remains for the people of God, as a receptive state, designed to enlarge and prepare the mind for the higher glories of the resurrection. The idea is certainly exceedingly pleasant and glorious. Shall this peaceful rest be ours? "Let us therefore fear, lest a promise being left us of entering into his rest, any of you should seem to come short of it," *Heb.* 4 : 1. "Let us labor to enter into that rest." *Heb.* 4 : 11.

DO THE DEPARTED REVISIT EARTH?

Another deeply interesting inquiry, respecting the departed during the intermediate state, is, are they permitted to revisit earth, and do they ever see or know us in our trials, and wanderings, and sins? The idea that this is the fact, is exceedingly pleasant *to some*, and it must be admitted that there are intimations in Scripture that their presence is possible, and that they have appeared to men. Moses and Elias appeared to Jesus and the three disciples, and one of the prophets was sent as a revelator to John.

But it becomes us to be cautious in the views we entertain on a subject of this nature. Our Lord never intended that we should, in any sense, supplicate the dead, or be distracted by superstitious views respecting their presence, so as to call our attention from life's appropriate duties. He would have us to be governed especially by the belief of his own immediate presence and inspection, and to live and act as seeing him who is invisible.

The melancholy cases of extravagance and lunacy, which have been caused by modern professed spiritual manifestations, show what would be the sad results, were God to suffer a conscious intercourse between the departed and the living, in our present weak and imperfect state. And as he does not suffer this intercourse, so he has not authorized us to believe in the general or uniform presence of departed friends. We are inclined to the belief that the departed are not present with or around about us. For to be constantly present, and to behold our sorrows, our wanderings, and our sins, and to be personally conversant with all the sad vicissitudes of time, would seem to be incompatible with that state of rest and delightful repose, which the people of God are said to enjoy with the Saviour. Nor can we suppose that such a constant intercourse would be agreeable to those who have been longing to escape from the very sight of earth's corruptions and vices. Angelic messengers may communicate to them, from time to time, such intelligence of the developments of God's wondrous plans of providence and love, as will be adapted to inspire them with hopes most ardent in respect to the future. But what we know not now, we shall know hereafter.

A DELIGHTFUL PROSPECT.

The views now presented are delightfully attractive. Though we shall not enter upon the promised—the full reward of the world to come, until the resurrection, yet, the intermediate state will have its peculiar and exalted joys. During all this period we shall be with Jesus—with him who from the beginning loved us, who died for us, and rose again. And what an attraction will this be to those who love him. Though Paul did not expect his crown until the day of Christ's glorious appearing, yet he felt that it was better, far better, to depart and be with Jesus, than to remain on earth. And so thousands of others have felt, who have been drawn heavenward by the power of his attractive love. In connection with his wondrous character as God, and the matchless and divine perfections which cluster around him, his amiableness, kindness, tenderness, purity and loveliness as Mediator, are sufficient to render his presence a sure guarantee of all that is blissful and joyous. Being the same yesterday, to-day, and forever, he possesses all the same lovely traits in his exalted position that he so winningly manifested in the days of his sojourn in the flesh. He is none the less meek and lowly in heart—none the less kind and affectionate in disposition, than when ministering to others good on earth. Cold and earthly, sensual and grovelling, and alienated must be that heart which never expands with delightful emotions in the prospect of being with Christ. And then, too, we shall be with him in delightful association with the gathered saints of all ages, waiting in ever-brightening hope for the redemption of their bodies, and the higher glories of the resurrection. And are there no attractions here? Think of that peaceful, quiet, holy repose, the souls of the just will enjoy, while patiently waiting in glorious anticipation for the kingdom of God. And we can well afford to wait for those higher glories of immortality ready to be revealed in the last time, in such society, and amidst such communings as will be with Jesus, and the just made perfect.

"There is a calm for those who weep,
A rest for weary _ilgrims found,
They softly lie, and sweetly sleep
With Jesus found.
The storm that wrecks the wintry sky,
No more disturbs their deep repose,
Than summer evening's latest sigh
That shuts the rose."

Vast revolutions may sweep over the world: the

demon of war may howl, and let loose his fury upon the nations, and drive his bloody chariot over the crushed victims of his cruelty—oceans may roll, and the warring elements of popular tumult join their forces in fearful storms—lightnings may blaze, and loud thunders utter their voices—but not all the revolutions or commotions of this lower world, or universe combined, can disturb the repose of the holy—the rest of the departed, shadowed forth in the silent and quiet sleep of the grave.

"To be delivered from trouble—to be relieved from oppressive power—to be freed from care and pain, from sickness and distress—to lie down as in a bed of security, in a long oblivion of our woes—to sleep in peace, without the fear of interruption—how pleasing is the prospect: how full of consolation!"

"Blessed are the dead that die in the Lord; yea, saith the Spirit, from henceforth, for they *rest* from their labors and their works do follow them."

CHAPTER IV.

THE RESURRECTION.

THE world to come, is clearly represented to us in Scripture as a world of progress, and infinite and glorious development. As in the present life, the physical and mental powers of man are successively developed, until the maturity of manhood is attained; so in the unfoldings of another life, in the kingdom of God, we shall be advanced from one stage of being to another, until we reach the summit of heaven's glory.

It is important that we should keep these different states, as presented in Scripture, distinct in our minds, and the promises appropriate to each, if we would form a correct and consistent idea of those things which God has revealed to us by his spirit.

A FUNDAMENTAL DOCTRINE.

The intermediate state, though rendered peaceful and blessed by the presence of Jesus, and hallowed by the associations of angels and redeemed spirits, cannot be compared to the glory which shall be revealed in us, at the appearing of Jesus Christ, and the resurrection of the just.

It is manifest from the uniform teachings of the apostles of our Lord, that the doctrine of the resurrection of the dead was in their estimation fundamental to the whole Christian system, and to all the hopes inspired by the Gospel.

Jesus repeatedly promised, "Ye shall be recompensed at the resurrection of the just." And the Apostle says, 1 *Cor.* 15 : 12–19, "Now, if Christ be preached that he rose from the dead, how say some among you that there is no resurrection of the dead? But if there be no resurrection of the dead, then is Christ not risen; and if Christ be not risen, then is our preaching vain, and your faith is also vain. Yea, and we are found false witnesses of God; because we have testified of God that he raised up Christ: whom he raised not up, if so be that the dead rise not. For if the dead rise not, then is not Christ raised; and if Christ be not raised, your faith is is vain; ye are yet in your sins. Then they also which are fallen asleep in Christ are perished."

No language could more strongly declare the essential importance of this doctrine to the whole Christian system than this, and its necessary connection with all our immortal hopes. In contemplating, therefore, the world to come, and in endeavoring to gain some idea of its superior attractions, we must be careful to give to this subject its revealed place and prominence in all our conceptions.

As the doctrine is often denied, and as generally

misunderstood, it is proposed for the confirmation of faith,—

1. To present the evidence which the Scriptures furnish in proof of the doctrine of the resurrection of our material bodies, and

2. To show that it is in harmony with reason and science; with our immortal and aspiring natures; with all the works of God, and opens before the believer a career of immortality inconceivably grand and glorious.

REVEALED IN THE OLD TESTAMENT.

In presenting the Scriptural evidence upon this subject, it must be confessed that but little is revealed respecting it in the Old Testament. And yet there are intimations given, which clearly show that the doctrine was known and cherished by saints of old, and was an object of that faith which invested the world to come, in their estimation, with attractions exceedingly joyous. In the Epistle to the Hebrews it is affirmed, that it was the hope of it which supported the martyrs for the Jewish religion. "And others were tortured, not accepting deliverance, that they might attain a better resurrection." *Heb.* 11 : 35.

The patriarch *Job* manifestly had reference to the resurrection of the body when he said, "Oh that my words were written! Oh that they were printed in a book! that they were graven with an iron pen and lead in the rock forever, *that I know* that my Redeemer liveth, and that he shall stand in the latter day upon the earth; and though after my skin worms destroy this body, yet in my flesh shall I see God; whom I shall see for myself, and mine eyes shall behold, and not another; though my reins be consumed within me?" These words have been the subject of much controversy; but the circumstances in which they were spoken, the solemnity of the introduction, and the devoted tone of the language, evidently point to something greater than a temporal deliverance.

The doctrine is also clearly taught in *Isaiah*, 25: 8, and 26: 19, "He will swallow up death in victory; and the Lord God will wipe away tears from off all faces; and the rebuke of his people shall he take away from off all the earth: for the Lord hath spoken it. Thy dead men shall live, together with my dead body shall they arise. Awake and sing, ye that dwell in dust: for thy dew is as the dew of herbs, and the earth shall cast out the dead."

That these words refer to the resurrection of the dead is decided by the Apostle Paul, who affirms that they shall be brought to pass, or be fulfilled, "when this corruptible shall have put on incorruption, and this mortal shall have put on immortality" 1 *Cor.* 15: 54.

It was also clearly and distinctly announced to the prophet *Daniel*, 12: 2, 13, "And many of them which sleep in the dust of the earth shall awake, some to everlasting life, and some to shame and everlasting contempt. But go thy way till the end be: *for thou shalt rest*, and stand in thy lot at the end of the days." This last declaration shows that the state intervening between death and the resurrection is one of rest, as shown in the previous chapter.

These Scriptures show conclusively that the resurrection of the dead was known and clearly apprehended by patriarchs and prophets. As Jesus Christ came, not only to save from sin, but to abolish death, and annul the curse incurred by the sin of man, it seems most probable, that in the promises of a Redeemer, made from the beginning, this one prominent part of the object of his mission was clearly announced for the confirmation of the faith and hope of the faithful. This view of the subject furnishes a rational exposition of the Scriptures quoted, and shows the ground of the faith of those who, in olden time, looked amid life's perils and miseries for a "better resurrection."

The position here taken is confirmed from the consideration, that the resurrection of the dead was not first revealed by Christ after his advent, but was distinctly known among the Jews at his appearing, and for centuries before. Thus, 175 years before the birth of our Saviour, it is related, in the apochryphal book of Maccabees, 7: 9, "that in the persecutions of Antiochus Epiphanes, Eleazer, a mother and her seven sons endured the most cruel torments with patience, and died in the assured hope of a glorious resurrection." "Thou, like a fury," said one of the sons, "takest us out of the present life, but the king of the world shall raise us up, who have died for his lous, unto everlasting life."

At the time of our Lord's appearance we find that the doctrine was held by the Pharisees, and is repeatedly referred to as a well-known truth among the Jews.

The opinion of some learned men that the doctrine of the transmigration of souls from one body to another, so commonly held in ancient times, and at the present day among the Indians and Chinese, is a perversion or corruption of the originally-revealed doctrine of the resurrection of the dead, is not improbable. Herodotus informs us, that the ancient Egyptians said, "That the soul of man is immortal, and that the body being corrupted, the soul goes into the body of one animal after another, and after it has gone round, or performed its circuit, through all terrestrial and marine animals and birds, it again entereth into some human body; and that this circumvolution was completed in three thousand years." Hence, no doubt, arose their efforts to preserve the bodies of the dead by embalming, and their costly tombs, hewn in, or built out of the imperishable rock, to secure them for future habitation. All this looks, indeed, like a corruption of the doctrine of the resurrection of the dead.

BROUGHT OUT TO A CLEARER LIGHT IN THE NEW TESTAMENT.

But this truth revealed as a glorious reality in the beginning, and perverted and corrupted by the folly and depravity of man, was indeed brought out to the light, and set forth in its own bright relation and consequences by the teachings of our Lord, and especially by his own triumphant resurrection and ascension. It is one of the great burdens of the New Testament Scriptures. It is taught—

1. By clear and repeated announcement—*John*, 5: 21, 25–29, "For as the Father raiseth up the dead, and quickeneth them; even so the son quickeneth whom he will. Verily, verily, I say unto you, the hour is coming, and now is, when the dead shall hear the voice of the Son of God; and they that hear shall live. For as the Father hath life in himself, so hath he given to the Son to have life in himself; and hath given him authority to execute judgment also, because he is the Son of Man. Marvel not at this: for the hour is coming in the which all that are in their graves shall hear his voice, and shall come forth; they that have done good unto the resurrection of life; and they that have done evil unto the resurrection of damnation."

No language could more clearly or strongly affirm, than this, the future resurrection of all the dead. Let it be noticed that it is that which is dead, in the grave, that is to hear the voice of the Son of Man, and live, and not the living spirit.

From the fact that our Lord says, that the hour is not only coming, *but now is*, when the dead hear his voice, some have argued that only a spiritual resurrection was here intended. But there is no ground or necessity in the passage for any such conclusion. Was it not a fact that at that hour or time, the dead did hear the voice of the Son of God and live? Did he not frequently, during his ministry, raise the dead to life? Did not Lazarus, and the son of the lone widow of Nain, and the daughter of Jairus, and others unnamed, hear the voice of the Son of God miraculously put forth, and live? Our Lord, therefore, in affirming that the dead at that time heard his voice, was only declaring what was everywhere, in Judea, known to be a fact. And to show his power to do all that he had said respecting the resurrection of the dead universally, he refers to these facts, which were at the time repeatedly occurring in answer to the voice of the Son of God, to illustrate his word.

John, 11 : 24, 25, "Martha saith unto him, I know that he shall rise again in the resurrection at the last day. Jesus said unto her, I am the resurrection and the life: he that believeth in me, though he were dead, yet shall he live."

John, 6 : 39, "And this is the Father's will which hath sent me, that of all which he hath given me, I should lose nothing, but should raise it up again at the last day."

Acts, 24 : 15, And have hope toward God, which they themselves also ~~abhor~~, that there shall be a resurrection of the dead, both of the just and the unjust."

Phil. 3 : 20, 21, "For our conversation is in heaven; from whence also we look for the Saviour, the Lord Jesus Christ, who shall change our vile body that it may be fashioned like unto his glorious body, according to the working whereby he is able even to subdue all things unto himself."

These passages show conclusively that the resurrection of the dead is one of the great and peculiar doctrines revealed in the gospel, as a part, and a very glorious part of that blessed hope which it inspires respecting our future destiny.

PROVED FROM THE RESURRECTION OF CHRIST.

The great argument presented in the New Testament in confirmation of this doctrine, and in illustration of the nature and glory of the resurrection of the dead, is the fact and nature of the resurrection of Christ. The apostle says, "But now is Christ risen from the dead, and become the first fruits of them that slept." 1 *Cor.* 15 : 20. And again, For our conversation is in heaven; from whence also we look for the Saviour, the Lord Jesus Christ: who shall change *our vile body* that it may be fashioned like unto his glorious or glorified body. *Phil.* 3 : 20.

These passages bring to our view an exceedingly interesting fact, and one, too, of most significant import. They not only assure us that the resurrection of Christ is a sure pledge of ours in their time, but that our resurrection bodies are to be of the same nature precisely as his. Our vile or corruptible bodies are to be fashioned like unto his glorified body. So that, if he rose in a spiritual body, we shall also; but if he rose in that same material body which was crucified, and laid in the tomb of Joseph of Arimathea, our resurrection will also be in material bodies.

This point can be definitely settled only by an appeal to Scripture testimony; and it is important that it should be attentively considered by all, who would form a scriptural estimate of the exceedingly glorious attractions of the resurrection state.

In the second chapter of John's gospel we are told that, on a certain occasion, when the Jews demanded of our Lord a sign in proof of his authority for doing what he did, He said, "Destroy this temple, and in three days I will raise it up." The Jews misunderstanding his reference, said, "Forty and six years was this temple"—the temple at Jerusalem—"in building, and wilt thou rear it up in three days?" "But he spake of the temple of his body. When, therefore, he was risen from the dead, his disciples remembered that he said this unto them; and they believed the Scriptures and the word which Jesus had said."

In this passage the question is put beyond all rational controversy, that our Lord, in predicting his own resurrection on the third day, had respect to his *material* body; for it was that which the Jews could and would destroy, that was to be raised up. The spiritual nature of Christ they could not touch or destroy—and hence, it was clearly not his spiritual body merely, which was predicted to rise, but his mortal, material body. All this is most fully illustrated and confirmed in the events that followed.

When Jesus said to the Jews, "Destroy this temple," this body of mine, "and in three days I will raise it up," he fully committed himself on a point most vital, from which there was no retreat, and in regard to which there was no room for evasion. The truth of his claims as the Messiah, was deliberately staked upon this single fact, that if they put him to death, as he knew they meditated, he would rise again to life, in that same body, on the third day. If he arose, then, agreeably to his own prediction, it would demonstrate his pretensions—if not, the failure would prove him an impostor.

This point, those who were instrumental in his death, well understood, and they determined to put his claims to the most rigid scrutiny. And hence we find this record, *Matt.* 27: 62–64. "Now the next day that followed the day of preparation, the chief priests and Pharisees came together unto Pilate, saying, sir, we remember that that deceiver said, while he was yet alive, *After three days I will rise again.* Command, therefore, that the sepulchre be made sure until the third day, lest his disciples come by night, and steal him away, and say unto the people, He is risen from the dead: so the last error shall be worse than the first."

Now, all this arrangement could have reference only to that body which had died, and it showed a determination to test the truth or falsehood of the Saviour's pretensions to the utmost, confident of a triumph over him whom they regarded with abhorrence.

A most critical period was now reached in the history of the eventful life of our Lord, and hence, when his dead body was laid in the tomb, and the stone which closed the door sealed—around that sepulchre the most wakeful suspicion prevailed, the most watchful vigilance was exercised, and every precaution was taken to guard that body, in order to decide the fact whether *that body, which died*, and was laid in the grave, should continue there lifeless, beyond the specified time, or rise to life again as predicted.

It was a time of deep anxiety and suspense. The powers of light and darkness all around were awake, and watching the result. The soldiers silently paraded about the tomb, and the chief priests and Pharisees, anticipating a triumph, awaited the issue with deep and anxious emotion. Hour after hour rolled away. The first and the second nights were passed, and all was still. But the third day came, and that temple which had been destroyed was rebuilt—that body which lay in the tomb was re-animated, and re-united to the immortal part which went with the soul of the penitent thief to paradise on the day of his death.

Of this there is the most ample proof in the several accounts given by the evangelists, appointed as witnesses of his resurrection.

Passing over a number of incontrovertible circumstances which demonstrate the resurrection of that *material body* of our Lord, which was crucified, and died, we will first notice his appearance to his disciples at Jerusalem, recorded in *Luke*, 24: 36–46.

He had appeared to two of the brethren on their way to Emmaus, and was made known to them in the breaking of bread. While these two, having returned to Jerusalem, were relating to the other disciples what things were done in the way, and how he was made known to them, Jesus himself suddenly stood in the midst of them, and said, "Peace be unto you." But they were terrified and affrighted, and supposed that they had seen a spirit. And he said unto them, Why are ye terrified? and why do thoughts arise in your hearts? Behold my hands and my feet, that it is I myself; handle me and see—for a spirit hath not flesh and bones as ye see me have. And when he had thus spoken, he showed them his hands and his feet, bearing the marks of the nails. And while they yet believed not for joy, and wondered, he said unto them, Have ye here any meat? And they gave him a piece of a broiled fish, and of a honey-comb, and he took it, and did eat it before them."

This is an exceedingly interesting passage, and one which demonstrates, by a series of facts, the reality of the resurrection of the material body of our Lord.

1. The disciples, affrighted, supposed it was a spirit they saw; but, to correct this impression, the risen Saviour exhorted them not to be troubled, but to come and satisfy themselves that he was not a spirit, by beholding his hands and his feet—the

very scars of the wounds which had been made by the piercing of the nails and the spear: showing that it was the same body that was crucified, that had been raised, and in no sense a merely spiritual, etherial, or sublimated substance.

2. The risen Saviour positively declared that he was not a spirit, but had a body with flesh and bones, as other men. "Behold my hands and my feet, that it is I myself: handle me, and see for a spirit hath not flesh and bones as ye see me have." He shows us here a distinction between a material body and spirit. A spirit hath not flesh and bones. It is something distinct from matter. But he, in his resurrection body, had flesh and bones, and, therefore, manifestly had a material body.

3. And then, further to demonstrate to them this great and fundamental fact, which he seemed anxious to impress upon them, that he was not a spirit, but had a material body, he said, "Have ye here any meat? And they gave him a piece of a broiled fish and a honey-comb, and he took it, and did eat it before them." Now the Lord did, in truth, eat this fish and honey-comb, or he did not. If he did not, he was guilty of practising upon them a gross deception, which it would be impious to impute to our Lord. But if he did eat them, it demonstrates that he had a material body, as really as before his crucifixion.

But Thomas, one of the eleven, was not with them when Jesus thus appeared. And when it was told him what had occurred, it was so wonderful and, to him, incredible, that he said, "Except I shall see in his hands the print of the nails, and put my finger into the print of the nails, and thrust my hand into his side, I will not believe." *John*, 20 : 25. Well, Jesus gave him, as he did the other disciples, this visible and sensible demonstration of his risen body.

John, 20 : 26, 29, "And after eight days, again his disciples were within, and Thomas with them: then came Jesus, the door being shut, and stood in the midst, and said, 'Peace be unto you.' Then saith he to Thomas, 'Reach hither thy finger, and behold my hands; and reach hither thy hand, and thrust it into my side; and be not faithless, but believing.' And Thomas answered, and said unto him, 'My Lord and my God.' Jesus saith unto him, 'Thomas, because thou hast seen me, thou hast believed: blessed are they which have not seen, and yet have believed.'"

Evidence could not be furnished more direct, or completely demonstrative than this, that the risen body of our Lord was the same material body as that which was crucified. The testimony given shows that it was a body which had flesh and bones —a body which could eat and drink, which could be handled with material hands, and which bore in it the marks of the nails and the spear made on Calvary.

This was the body of our Lord which was glorified, and with this he ascended on high, in presence of his chosen witnesses. That any further change ever passed upon his body after his ascension, rendering it spiritual in distinction from matter, or more etherial and sublimated than it was when handled by the disciples, we have no warrant to affirm in Scripture. The clear import of Scripture is, that he did not and never will put off that material part of our nature, which he has taken into an indissoluble and eternal union with himself.

In determining, therefore, that the resurrection body of our Lord was material, we have decided the nature of our own resurrection bodies. For, says the apostle, "Now is Christ risen from the dead, and become the first fruits or earnest of them that sleep." His resurrection is a proof and pledge, and an illustration of that of others, which could not be, were his not of the same nature and character as all others. This point is still more definitely settled by a passage already quoted, *Phil.* 3 : 21, "For our conversation is in heaven; from whence also we look for the Saviour, the Lord Jesus Christ: who shall change our vile body that it may be fashioned like unto his glorious body."

In this passage the pattern is given, according to which our bodies are to be fashioned at the resurrection. It has been shown that the raised and glorified body of our Lord was material; and it is therefore demonstrated that ours will also be material.

THE REANIMATION OF THAT WHICH DIES.

The doctrine of the resurrection of our material bodies, is still further confirmed, from the consideration, that it is the uniform testimony of Scripture, that it is that which dies, that is to be quickened or made alive. The prophet *Daniel* says, "And many of them that sleep *in the dust of the earth*, or in the grave, shall awake." Our Lord says, "Marvel not at this: for the hour is coming, in which *all that are in the graves* shall hear his voice, and shall come forth." The Apostle *Paul*, in answering the question in 1 *Cor*. 15 : 35, "How are the dead raised up, and with what bodies do they come?" says, "Thou fool, that which thou sowest is not quickened," or made alive, "except it die"—thus showing that there can be no resurrection of the dead except in respect to those who have died. Without multiplying quotations, it may confidently be affirmed to be the uniform testimony of Scripture, that it is that which dies which is to be raised up. If so, then it must be the material body; for no other ever dies. The spiritual nature or body of man does not, and cannot die, and therefore it cannot be quickened or raised from the dead. It must then be the material body which is to rise. The argument from Scripture on this point is conclusive and irrefutable. Let us turn now to other considerations which strikingly corroberate and sustain the view taken.

BODY ESSENTIAL TO MIND.

The resurrection of our material bodies from the grave, is undoubtedly purely a Scriptural doctrine. And yet in the light which the Divine Word sheds upon this subject, a presumptive argument may be drawn in its favor from the wonderful mechanism and powers of the human body. The mechanism of the human frame is exceedingly curious, and intricately wonderful. The body is a temple or dwelling-place of the immortal mind, and was designed as a combination of instruments through which its development and external manifestation was to be made to the world, and its divinely-derived powers exercised. Now, the wonderful powers of the human body, and its wisely and nicely-adjusted adaptation to the faculties and destiny of the mind, seem clearly to indicate that its existence will be necessary to the full development of mind in a future world, and to its highest welfare.

1. Consider what astonishing and wonderful powers the members of the body possess, as instruments of the soul, as manifested in all the beautiful, the useful, the noble, and grand productions of mechanical art, as seen in the world. Who rears the beautiful mansion, the gorgeous temple, and adorns them with all their splendid and architectural members and proportions? Who forms and puts together the complicated, the highly-finished and nicely-adjusted parts of a steam-engine, and other machinery by which the elements of nature are appropriated to the use of man, and by which the most beautiful and astonishing results are produced? By what agency has the magnetic telegraph been constructed, by which the lightning is made to answer to the call of man, and to furnish a highway of

thought for the nations? The answer is, these are the products of the human mind, accomplished by the instrumentalities of the members of the human body. The mind conceived and devised these combinations of wisdom, utility and beauty, but the mind could never have executed its conceptions, or have given form to its ideas in external nature, had it not been for its mechanical agent the body, furnished for its use by the Great Creator.

In every triumph of mechanical art we see not only the manifestations of active intellect, but the wonderful powers and adaptations of the human body to all the conceptions and combinations of the ever-active and aspiring mind. It is manifest that the body is now necessary to the development and highest achievements of mind, and essential to its welfare and happiness. Will it not be so hereafter? Will not the mind need a body, with powers similar to those now possessed, refined and augmented, as its minister or agent in the execution of those wonderful schemes which will be devised and enjoyed in its enlarged and eternal development? Will the mind, in a future world, be able to do its will, and accomplish its pleasure independently of a body as now possessed, and better attain the high destinies of its being? Certainly we are not warranted in such a conclusion, by anything we can see within or about us in the present world.

The body, with its various mechanical organs and powers, is now essential to the progress and achievements of mind. What could the spirit do without it? What execute of good or evil? Now, the fact that the body is so essential to the operations of mind in the present world, seems clearly to indicate that a body must be essential to its highest well-being in any world. And this truth the Scriptures declare in the doctrine of the resurrection; and hence it may be seen that the doctrine is natural, and in accordance with the nature and wants of the mind.

But if the mind, as some suppose, will rise to a higher state of perfection when emancipated from the body—if it will then be free from all that impedes and clogs its upward progress, why was it ever connected with a body? Is it not an impeachment, virtually, of the wisdom and goodness of the Creator, to say that the body, as such, is a clog to the mind, and that it will better attain its highest end when disconnected with matter? A body diseased and corrupted, and enfeebled by sinful indulgence, may utterly fail to accomplish the high end designed in connection with the mind, and does undoubtedly therefore hinder and defeat that progress which might otherwise have been made. But this disastrous result is not to be attributed to the body. Would such have been the result had no sin or disease ever have corrupted or enfeebled the body? We repeat the inquiry, why, according to the unnatural and unproved assertion, that the body —or a body—impedes the mind, did God form for man a material body, with such wonderful mechanical powers, and associate it essentially with the mind in all its present pursuits, probation, and enjoyments?

Did he do it that he might simply dash it in pieces as a vile vessel at death? or only that in it he might imprison and impede, afflict and torment the Spirit? How unreasonable!

In many cases the association of mind with the body in this life answers no valuable purpose. How many die in infancy and childhood! How many by bodily disease and deformity suffer! Did God make these in vain? It would seem that he did, or what is worse, only that they might be tormentors, if they are not to live hereafter. Now, there is no way in which we can conceive that the goodness and wisdom of God can be vindicated in the construction of the human form, and its essential association with mind, but on the ground of the Scriptural doctrine—that he intended the body to be as immortal as the mind, and its eternal associate and helper. Had man never sinned, according to the clearly-implied teachings of Scripture, his body would have lived on in immortal bloom as long as his mind.

But sin for a time has interrupted the order of heaven, and death has entered our world. But the second Adam will restore the ruins of the first, and re-establish the union of mind and body in an ever-endeared, immortal, and glorious form.

THE HIGHER ADAPTATIONS OF THE BODY.

But there are other and higher powers of the human body than those which have been named; which also seem clearly to intimate its high and glorious destiny. How wonderful, for example, are the powers of eloquence! What vast multitudes have been charmed and enchanted, and swayed to and fro as the trees of the forest before the tempest, by the eloquence of such men as Demosthenes and Cicero in ancient times, and in modern times by such men as Whitefield and a Patrick Henry! And yet there have been, and are now, multitudes in the world equally as eminent in their sphere as these.

Now, all this power of eloquence is not merely the effect of mind: for would the mind be thus eloquent, and produce these thrilling effects independently of the body? surely not. To produce this effect the lungs heave, the muscles of the throat contract and dilate—the tongue moves obedient to the will—the lips open or are compressed—the countenance beams—the eye brightens and sparkles with emotion—and the whole body moves and gestures the sentiments and passions of the soul. Could the mind, then, be eloquent without a body? All these things go to show the wonderful powers of the body, and its perfect adaptation to the nature, and desires, and designs of the presiding spirit. The mind certainly could not fulfil its destiny in life without the body.

Can it do without these aids and powers in another life? Who that was authorized has ever said it can? All the analogies of nature then, in harmony with the doctrine of the resurrection, seem to indicate the necessity of a material body to the highest welfare and development of the immortal mind.

And then, too, see the power of music, performed through material organs, to charm, and elevate, and enrapture the soul. How sweet are human voices tuned to harmony and love! The powers of a Jenny Lind, and a Madam Sontag, show what human voices can do, and what they may become under favorable circumstances. What thousands hang in ecstasy upon the thrilling notes which warble from their throats! How strangely wonderful that organism which can produce such varied, pleasing, and exciting effects! And yet, no doubt, there are thousands equally gifted in the wide world, unknown and uncultivated; for,—

> "Full many a gem of purest ray serene,
> The dark unfathomed caves of ocean bear:
> Full many a flower is born to blush unseen,
> And waste its sweetness on the desert air."

Will their sweetness never be known? Will they not in another life exhale their fragrance? They will, according to the doctrine of the resurrection. And if such thrilling effects can be produced by music on earth, performed through material organs, oh, what will be the music of that great multitude which no man can number, around the throne, whose voices in the resurrection state will, as now, be the result of material organization, tuned to sweetest harmony and love, as it comes over the soul as the rushing of mighty waters, or as the whispers of gentlest zephyrs! Is such music as can be procured through material organization, and material things, only to be known and heard in a world of sin? Can it be that this bodily organism, capable of such wonderful effects, is only destined to live during life's short years of suffering and trial? Or does not rather nature intimate that a body so marvellous in its construction, and so wisely adapted to the uses and desires of the mind, should live and accompany the immortal spirit in all its eternal progress?

All these considerations must clearly show the entire harmony of the doctrine of the resurrection of our material bodies, as taught in Scripture, with the nature of the human soul, and its highest development and welfare. And this harmony and adaptation might be further argued from the exquisite arrangement and power of the nervous system to communicate the most intense pleasure to the soul, as is often experienced, and from the activity of all the senses in bringing the mind into immediate communication with the perfections of God, manifested in the boundless material universe. But further we cannot now go. The theme is a delightful one, and is adapted to shadow forth the transcendent attractions of the resurrection state.

A PHYSIOLOGICAL OBJECTION ANSWERED.

To the resurrection of our material bodies there are some common objections constantly urged by the unbelieving, which it will be important to consider, before noticing more extendedly the glories, and immortal results of the doctrine.

Our bodies die, and are in the course of dissolution resolved into their original elements. Often the substances of which they are composed are scattered, and borne in fragments and particles to widely different parts of the earth; and in the processes of nature enter again and again into the composition of vegetable and animal bodies indefinitely. Now, from this, unbelievers have maintained that it is an utter impossibility and absurdity, that the dead should be raised, whose bodies have been dissolved, dissipated, and formed into countless new combinations. But this objection rests upon a false assumption in regard to what is necessary to constitute personal identity, and a perverted view of the teachings of Scripture. It supposes that all, and the very same particles of matter which compose our bodies when they die, must necessarily be gathered up from their wide dispersion through the world, and extracted from every other combination, vegetable, animal, or human, into which they may have entered, and be reconstructed, if the dead are ever raised. But as some of the substances which composed the body of one man, when he died, may have entered into the bodies of others when they died, the resurrection of the self-same body is regarded as utterly impossible.

But the Scriptures do not teach that the same particles of matter in all respects will enter into our future bodies, or be at all necessary to the resurrection. When they declare that the dead will be raised, they use the language of common life, and mean that our raised bodies will be the bodies that died, in the same sense that our bodies are the same at different periods of our lives. When it is said that a man has the same body now that he had twenty years ago, nothing absurd, or that is contrary to consciousness is uttered. Every one feels and believes that he has at all times the same body in a popular sense, however great the change produced by waste or supply. It bears every scar, or mark, or deformity, once made permanently upon it. And yet it is well known that, philosophically speaking, a man has not a body composed of the same particles at any two distinct periods of his life. But yet a full knowledge of this does not alter his consciousness that he is always the same being, in body as well as soul. At one period of a man's life, he is in the bloom of health, and then in a short time he is reduced by disease to a mere skeleton, and then again the return of health clothes him with new flesh and vigor. And yet through all these changes, he feels and knows that he has the same body, as a matter of consciousness, and in accordance with the language of common life.

It is supposed that our bodies, by waste and accretion, undergo an entire change once in seven years. And yet have I not the same body I had seven years ago? I feel that I am myself, and recognize my body as the same, whatever changes may have taken place. Now, the sum of all this is, *that the same identical particles of matter are not necessary at all times to constitute personal identity.* Any human form may throw off, by piecemeal, the whole of the matter contained in its formation, and take to itself new substances of the same kind, and according to the same laws of organization, in connection with the same mind, and still preserve its personai identity. All this we know to be true.

So in the resurrection, it will not be necessary that all the same substances should enter into the raised bodies, which were in them at death, to constitute them the same. This the Scriptures abundantly declare, and they are thus in harmony with constantly observed facts in physiology. In 1 Cor. 15, the apostle Paul teaches most definitely that our resurrection bodies will not be composed of all the same particles of matter as in the present life.

PAUL'S VIEW OF PERSONAL IDENTITY

In answer to the question, "How are the dead raised up, and with what bodies do they come?" He says, "Thou fool, that which thou sowest is not quickened except it die; and that which thou sowest, thou sowest not that body which shall be, but it bears grain; it may chance of wheat or some other grain. But God giveth it a body as it hath pleased him, and to every seed his own, or its own body;" that is, he gives to wheat the body of wheat, to corn the body of corn, and so from whatever kind of seed is sown there springs a like body.

The apostle does not intend to say that there is a perfect analogy between grain sown, and human bodies buried in the grave; but he does mean to teach, that as from grain sown, and which dies in the ground, there springs another body or grain of the same kind, though not containing the same particles of matter: so from our dead bodies, buried in earth, there will at the resurrection spring another body of the same kind, and containing, perhaps, enough of the old body to form the basis of the new. "It is, perhaps, a twentieth part of a grain of wheat which is sown and dies in the ground, which springs up and forms a part of the new grain; the rest rots in the ground and remains. It is not needed in the new body which God gives the wheat, and is not called forth again. So we are taught, our bodies which die will not be the same, as to particles of matter, as those which arise." Old particles will be dropped, and, for aught we know, new ones assumed, in that wonderful change which is to fit us for the high destinies in reserve.

If, then, all the same particles of matter which constitute our present bodies, do not or will not enter into our future bodies, the argument against the resurrection, founded upon the assumption that they will, and that they cannot be gathered up, entirely fails; for they are not necessary to accomplish all that the Scriptures predict.

Admitting, then, that large portions of the human body after death do enter into the composition of other living bodies, in such a manner as to render it impossible to gather them up, to reincorporate them into the new ones, the whole difficulty vanishes at once on the Scriptural doctrine that all the same particles will not be raised. As God can give to the wheat a new body, and yet it be wheat still, possessing the same nature as the old, so he can in the resurrection, if need be, give men bodies, and yet preserve our personal identity.

If any portion of the old body will be necessary to form the basis or nucleus of the new, in order to constitute it in every sense the same, it cannot be proved that enough may not be retained from the composition of other bodies to answer this purpose. "The human body, as that of all other animals, is composed of the same substances as those which constitute large and essential parts of the mineral kingdom,—nitrogen, oxygen, carbon, and hydrogen, potash, soda, phosphorus, sulphur, lime, and iron." Now, may not a small portion of these gaseous or solid substances be preserved, by the power of God, so as to form the basis of the new body? And if there could not, a body composed of these substances, under the same organization, and in connection with the same individual mind, would be the same body in Scripture language. It is obvious, therefore, that no facts in physiological science are contradicted, by the doctrine of the resurrection of our material bodies.

A WONDERFUL TRANSFORMATION.

The Scriptures teach that our resurrection bodies will not only not contain all the matter they now do, but that, in many respects, they will be very different from what they now are, and far more beautiful and glorious. They will pass through a wonderful transformation, in their resurrection and transition to immortal glory. This is clearly and beautifully illustrated in the apostle's description. He says of the body, "It is sown in corruption, it is raised in incorruption: it is sown in dishonor, it is raised in glory: it is sown in weakness, it is raised in power; it is sown a natural body, it is raised a spiritual body." And again he says, "Behold, I show you a mystery: we shall not all sleep, but we shall all be changed, in a moment, in the twinkling of an eye, at the last trump: for the trumpet shall sound, and the dead shall be raised incorruptible, and we shall be changed. For this corruptible must put on incorruption, and this mortal must put on immortality."

This language certainly denotes a most wonderful and glorious change in the raised bodies, yet not such as to destroy our conscious and acknowledged identity.

1. "*It is sown in corruption.*" All the tendencies

of the body at death, are to loathsome corruption and dissolution. In life we are subject to disease and decay, and our dead we are compelled to bury out of our sight. But it will be raised in incorruption. It will then be so changed, that it will be no longer subject to disease, decay, and death.

2. "*It is sown in dishonor.*" It is laid in the grave an unsightly object, and it dies as a malefactor under the righteous sentence of heaven. But in the resurrection, it will be exceedingly beautiful. *It will be raised in glory.* It will be fashioned like unto Christ's glorious body, and made resplendent with his beauty. As God forms the diamond so beautiful from charcoal, the blackest of substances, so he will, of the corruptible and inglorious body, form one in the resurrection, surpassingly beautiful, and resplendently glorious.

3. "*It is sown in weakness.*" And how exceedingly weak it is! How incapable of resisting the attacks of disease, or the thousand agents at work for its destruction! How the strong man bows and sinks, a helpless thing, into the embraces of the tomb! Surely it is sown in weakness; but *it will be raised in power.* In the raised state, it will, no doubt, be endowed with marvellous powers—with the power of resisting all evil—with vastly increased powers of locomotion—with powers fully adequate to all the wants, and energies, and pure desires of the aspiring mind. It will know fatigue no more, nor exhaustion, and will not need to be invigorated by sleep and tender care.

4. "*It is sown a natural body.*" It is now a body possessed of many merely animal instincts and sensual propensities and appetites. It hungers and thirsts, and is subject to many vile affections and lusts, by which the mind is often degraded and enslaved. But not so in the resurrection. It will be raised a spiritual body—that is, a body freed from all merely animal and degrading propensities, entirely adapted to the wants and pursuits of the mind, which is spiritual, and wholly under its control. It will hence, in a very high and important sense, be a spiritual body, perfectly adapted to, and subservient to spirit, and no longer under the dominion of the flesh. Hence, we are assured by the Saviour, that in the resurrection, we shall neither marry nor be given in marriage, but shall be all as the angels of God, and equal one to another.

THE IMPORT OF A SPIRITUAL BODY.

From the fact, that in the resurrection, our bodies are to be spiritual, some have argued that they would no longer be material. But this cannot be true; for it has already been shown that they must and will be material. The term spiritual is not used here in opposition to material, but to that which is merely natural or animal. The phraseology of the passage shows conclusively that this spiritual body is material still; for, let it be noticed, it is the corruptible body that is changed into the incorruptible; the loathsome, dishonored body that becomes the beautiful and glorious; the weak which is changed into the powerful; and the natural body which we now have, that rises to the spiritual; for, says the apostle, "we must all be changed." But there is no evidence that God ever does, or can change matter into spirit. We know of but two substances in the universe, matter and mind, and what is not one must be the other.

The fact that it is this corruptible, natural body, we now have, which is changed into the spiritual, shows that the spiritual body cannot be spirit. It is a body denominated spiritual, we judge, because it will be adapted in a high degree to spirit. Freed from all merely animal and grovelling propensities, it will become subservient pre-eminently and only to the higher destinies of the immortal mind. It will be material still after its transformation, only in a state of higher perfection than we now possess. The resurrection body of our Lord was no doubt spiritual, and yet we have seen that it was material, having the distinctive properties of matter, and bearing about in it the infallible marks that it was the same that was crucified. And the Scriptures give us no intimation that his body was changed from matter to spirit, at his ascension. Now, as our *vile bodies* are to be changed, and fashioned like unto his body which was glorified, it is certain that they must be material.

A body entirely subservient to mind, and the minister only of its holy and benevolent purposes, may, with great propriety, be called a spiritual body. And such may be the control of the spirit over the body in the resurrection state, that it may transport it, at will, from place to place, or from world to world, as our Lord seemed to have conveyed his, without the usual slow process of locomotion.

Again, the Apostle assures us, "That flesh and blood cannot inherit the kingdom of God." From this, some have supposed that material bodies, such as the Saviour had after his resurrection, cannot enter heaven. But there are many forms and modifications of matter which are not flesh and blood, and therefore, the declaration that flesh and blood, as they are now constituted, unchanged and unpurified, cannot inherit the kingdom of God, does not assert that material bodies, in some form, may not enter. Let these vile bodies be so changed that they shall no longer be flesh and blood, and the apostolic declaration will no longer apply.

But the connection in which these words are found, and the qualifying and explanatory exposition given, shows what the apostle meant, and that he had no idea of teaching that our bodies would not be material as much so as they are now.

He says, "Now this I say, brethren, that flesh and blood cannot inherit the kingdom of God; neither doth corruption inherit incorruption. Behold I show you a mystery: we shall not all sleep (or die,) but we shall all be changed, in a moment, in the twinkling of an eye, at the last trump: for the trumpet shall sound, and the dead shall be raised incorruptible, *and we shall be changed.* For this corruption must put on incorruption, and this mortal must put on immortality. So when this corruption shall have put on incorruption, and this mortal shall have put on immortality, then shall be brought to pass the saying that is written; Death is swallowed up in victory. O death, where is thy sting? O grave where is thy victory? The sting of death is sin; and the strength of sin is the law; but thanks be to God, who giveth us the victory, through our Lord Jesus Christ."

Now, is it not most manifest from this description of the apostle, that he did not contemplate the laying aside of the material body, *but only its change* from mortal to immortal, from corruption to incorruption? He meant to say that flesh and blood as now constituted, or the human body, in its present gross, mortal, and corruptible state, would not partake of the pure and refined pleasures of an immortal, incorruptible state. To fit it for this, it must undergo a change according to the order of God's arrangement, in order to adapt it to its higher and more glorious sphere of being and employment. It is clear that the apostle meant nothing more than this; for he says, "that when this corruptible shall have put on incorruption, and this mortal shall have put on immortality, then shall be brought to pass the saying that is written, Death is swallowed up in victory. O death, where is thy sting? O grave, where is thy victory? Now, if it is not the material body that is raised, then there is no triumph over death and the grave. Death holds all he ever gets, and the greedy grave continues to sway his cruel sceptre over the generations of the dead forever. This exulting and triumphant language can have force only in application to the resurrection of that material body which dies. In its resurrection, a change will be produced in it miraculously, by the power of God, to fit it for a higher sphere; but it will be material still, and may have *flesh and bones*, as our Lord had after his resurrection, if it has not *flesh and blood* as in its present corruptible and mortal constitution.

EMBLEMS IN NATURE.

We have in nature many emblems of the transformation of our mortal bodies, which strikingly and beautifully illustrate the changes through which a body may pass, in fitting it for a higher sphere of being, without changing its material nature, or destroying its identity. Innumerable worms, and the loathsome caterpillar, which we would, perhaps, shudder to touch, creeping beneath our feet, are, in in their season, transformed from the larva to the beautiful chrysalis, and thence to the gaudy butterfly; whence they rise to a new sphere of life, subsistence, and enjoyment, winging their way over smiling nature, and sipping at every flower which God has opened for their pleasure. Now, these worms are just as much material in their higher state of development, as in their lower; and were they endowed with memory and intelligence, they would, no doubt, feel conscious that they were the same beings through all their changes.

So, in the resurrection, we may pass through just as great changes, as the caterpillar, and still preserve our materiality and conscious identity. In that change from mortal to immortal, from corruption to incorruption, from weakness to power, which is to fit us for our higher sphere of being; our bodies may be as much more beautiful than they are now, as the butterfly is than the caterpillar; and our powers of locomotion and our sphere of enjoyment may as greatly transcend those now possessed, if not infinitely more so, as do those of the soaring butterfly, the crawling worm. In view then of these considerations, what is there unnatural, unreasonable, and undesirable in the resurrection of our material bodies?

THE WORLD'S CEMETERY.

One more objection we must notice before we close this part of our subject. A correspondent of the New-York Evangelist notices an article in a number of the Democratic Review, presenting certain objections to the received doctrine of the resurrection of the body, which, as it is not long, we will transcribe:

"The statements to which we have referred are the following:—Now, if a resurrection of all who have lived should take place, even within a short time, without even any material increase of the vast number who have lived upon the earth, where would they find room, even for the shortest space of time, to dwell in? Their numbers would cover the whole surface of the earth in one solid mass, to the depth or heigth of miles in thickness.'—p. 244. "And again, according to computation on the subject, there has already existed on the earth a sufficient number of inhabitants to constitute a bulk of matter equal in amount to the whole contents of this globe, which amount will increase as time rolls on, until it may exceed it by ten-thousand fold."—p. 223.

"These are grave statements; let us see what they amount to when weighed in the balance of a just and undeniable demonstration. The flood, which emptied the earth of its inhabitants, took place in the year of the world 1656. The whole number of the human race previous to that period, and on all the earth would not exceed in round numbers to more than as many millions, and probably not half that number. But we will put it down at 1,556,000,000. Since the flood, there have been, say 4,200 years; that is, forty-two centuries. Now, it is supposed that the earth changes its population three times in a century. There have been, then, one hundred and twenty-six generations since the days of Noah. There are at present upon the earth's surface, according to the most accurate accounts 1,000,000,000 of inhabitants. But as this number diminishes in proportion as you turn back towards the days of Noah, it is unquestionably above and beyond the truth, to say that five hundred millions is the mean number that have been upon the earth since the day that Noah came out of the ark. This sum is to be multiplied by one hundred and twenty-six, the number of generations since that period, which gives in round numbers 63,000,000,000. This sum, added to that which had been upon the earth previous to the flood, gives 64,656,000,000. But we will call the whole, in round numbers, 65,000,000,000.

"We will next determine how many can be buried on a square rod, or sixteen and a half feet square. Taking the human race as they die, of different sizes, there can be at least one hundred and thirty; for we are at liberty to lay them in any position, so that one shall not overlay, or lie on another. Well, then, we place each body on its side. We will take from the square rod a strip, six and a half feet in width, on which we will lay persons of that height, the head of the one to the feet of the other. In this position it is demonstrable, that at least sixteen might lie in that course through. We will next take a strip five feet wide—we will place the bodies of persons of that height in the same position—and on this course we shall find it easy to lay at least twenty. Next, we will take a strip three feet wide, on which placing of this size, in the same position, we can place as many as thirty. In the remaining strip of two feet wide, we can place as many as seventy, of children, and a large proportion of the human race die in childhood. These, added together, make the number one hundred and thirty-six, but we will put it down at one hundred and thirty to every square rod. Now, there are one hundred and sixty square rods in an acre, therefore, on a square acre we might bury 20,800; but we will put it at 20,000 per acre. There are six hundred and forty square acres in every square mile; therefore in every square mile we could bury 12,800,000. The State of New York contains 46,000 square miles. This sum multiplied by the number just given, 12,800,000, or that which can be placed on every square mile, gives 558,800,000,000. But we found only 65,000,000,000 on the earth since the days of Adam. According to this, the territory of the Empire State would make something over *nine* burying grounds for the whole world! And if you place the bodies in their usual position as they are buried, the State of New York would furnish land enough for at least two cemeteries for the entire race of men.

"Alas, for the Review! How this statement, which cannot be questioned, for figures cannot lie, looks by the side of the declaration, that there had been enough already on the earth to form a body approximating in size to the earth itself. We heard the statement made, not long since, by a gentleman whom we had supposed incapable of committing such an error, that there had been a sufficient number on the earth to cover the land at least four feet deep.

"This statement was made on a funeral occasion, while dwelling upon the resurrection. We are inclined to think if his eye shall fall on the above solution or result, call it what you please, he will 'review' his sermon somewhat severely before he preaches it again."

Most of the objections brought against this and kindred doctrines, are equally unfounded, and foolish as the one just noticed.

FIRST GLORIOUS RESULT.

The doctrine of the resurrection of our material bodies, as presented in Scripture, is one so peculiarly beautiful and glorious, and invests our future life with attractions so unspeakable, that it seems to us surprising that any should wish to refute or deny it. Let us look at some of its glorious and manifold results.

One of the most obvious consequences of the resurrection of our material bodies will be, that we shall be forever connected with the material universe—with all those wonderful works of God, illimitable and unsearchable, which exist in the universe around us; and this, too, under circumstances most favorable for improvement and boundless enjoyment. Our bodies will be material bodies, rendered immortal, incorruptible, beautiful, and glorious; with all the senses complete and perfect, and in full exercise, and all under the control of a holy mind.

Our minds are now too generally the servants of the body. Too often all their noble faculties and powers are enslaved by a degrading sensuality, or by the necessary wants and cravings of our now mortal and weak natures. But in the resurrection it will not be so. It is easy to conceive of the reverse of all this, when every sense, and faculty, and power shall become wholly subservient to the highest intellectual and moral enjoyment; when the eye shall not only bring to our knowledge everything that is beautiful in the visible universe, but be employed as an instrument in making observations upon God's glorious works, from those mighty orbs which roll unnumbered around us, down to the smallest insect; and from the mysterious laws which bind suns and planets into harmonious systems and motions, down to the hidden principles which govern universal nature in all its productions—when the ear shall not only listen, with enraptured emotion, to the melody and harmony of sweet sounds, and exulting music, as it bursts from the swelling anthems of the redeemed; but shall be a means of social intercourse, of the reception of knowledge and enjoyment, and endless improvement—when the tongue, no longer an unruly member, full of deadly poison, shall be a means of conveying to others the pure sentiments of the soul, the knowledge we have acquired, and the discoveries we have made, as well as an instrument by which we shall join in the music of heaven, and speak forth the praises of Jehovah. And so all other senses developed, or as yet undeveloped, under the control of a holy mind, and in connection with the material universe, may be employed in the highest pursuits and purest enjoyments.

All this flows necessarily as a consequence, from the nature of our resurrection. And it is easy to see that the Scriptural view of this doctrine, placing us thus in connection with the material universe, under the most favorable and exalted circumstances, gives to our future existence a reality and a substantiality which no other view can, and opens before the mind visions of glory, inconceivably grand and magnificent. It does not separate us from matter, and all the loved forms and objects of the material universe, as do most merely spiritual theories, and place us in communication with a world of ghosts, of phantasies, and phantasms; but it brings us into certain connection, and identifies us, with God's glorious universe, the delighted spectators of his mighty works, and the students of his vast plans, as brought to view in the heavens which declare his glory. It is denied by many that spirits in another life have any knowledge of, or connection with, material things. We can neither affirm or deny anything certainly in respect to this; for we do not know. The agency of angels in the affairs of our world, proves nothing, for it may be that they have some kind of material organization, by which and through which they exert their powers. The manner and form of their appearance, as recorded in Scripture, always in the form of men, favors the idea that they have refined material bodies. But be this as it may, we are certain that the resurrection of our material bodies, brings us into a real and tangible connection with the works of God as described.

SECOND GLORIOUS RESULT.

This leads to another remark and consequence of the resurrection, which is, that our knowledge of God, and of his attributes, will be acquired in a future state as now, for the most part through the work of his hands. It is manifest that we have now no knowledge of God, which was not derived principally through the medium of sensation, from our contact and intercourse with the material world. Whatever God has been pleased to reveal in his Word, has a direct reference to his works, or to the objects and operations of nature, by and through which his incomprehensible perfections are exhibited. And when he would reveal to us his moral character more clearly, and commend more attractively his love, he did it not simply by abstract announcement, but by manifesting himself in the flesh, and thus seeking through the medium of a material body to illustrate himself to his creatures.

Is it not true, therefore, that the clearest, brightest views we have of God, or that creatures have ever enjoyed, are those of "God manifest in the flesh." And how tender, affecting, and soul-cheering is the knowledge and condescension here communicated! Even the angels, who have stood in the immediate presence of the Creator, here bend with adoring wonder, to search into the wonders of God, revealed no where else so mysteriously and affectingly. In what other way could the Infinite and Invisible so clearly and becomingly have made himself known? It seems, therefore, certain that all correct knowledge of God and his attributes is now derived, in some form, from his works, or through material form, and all our ideas of him are materialized, being clothed in drapery drawn from the external world. Do we know that there is any correct knowledge of God which is not thence attained? Now, according to the doctrine of the resurrection, the same will be true hereafter. In all our employments, investigations, and enjoyments in a future world, we shall be constantly concerned with material objects, as well as conversant with spiritual things. Here will then exist a most striking resemblance between our present and our future existence. The one will be but the continuation of the other, in a higher and purer state than any on earth have ever conceived. Nor is there anything unreasonable in all this. It is all in entire harmony with the nature and capacities of the mind, and with the works of God in their adaptation to the mind through a material body. And it is highly probable, if not certain, that our bodies will be as necessary to the full development and action of the mind in a future life as here. To accomplish all that God has designed in our creation, we shall need the aid of all our senses and bodily members, or God would never raise the dead, as it is predicted he will. The doctrine of the resurrection, then, is in entire harmony with all that we can now see or know, of God and his designs, and with our immortal aspirings.

And what a field for seeing and hearing, for thought, action, and enjoyment, will God's boundless universe open to us in the resurrection state. Suppose our bodies were now free from all disease, infirmity, or imperfection, and rendered incapable of corruption, pain, weakness or fatigue, and were endowed with the power of ascending, by the will of God, to any world to see the wonders of Godhead there displayed, or to speed our way on some mission of love to some distant orb, would not this be a glorious prospect? And with a God to minister to our wants, and to direct our career, what higher perfection or felicity could we desire, were we holy or perfect as our Father in heaven is perfect.

THIRD GLORIOUS RESULT.

Another result of the resurrection of our material bodies will be, that our bodies which have been associated with us in all our trials and conflicts, and sufferings in life, will share with us all the rewards of the world to come; and all the dear forms which we have here loved, rendered glorious and immortal, will still be embraced in bonds of sweetest friendship and love.

All this would seem to be only a matter of justice. Through life the body has been the companion of the mind, and has been associated with it in all its probation, and in all its pursuits of righteousness or unrighteousness in training it for the destiny for which it is fitted. And is it not right that it should share with it in that destiny? Does not justice seem to demand that the two which have been united on earth should be indissolubly united in the world to come, and mutual sharers in its rewards?

The beings, then, that shall inhabit the future world will be no mere ghosts or spirits, whom no one can touch or embrace. Theirs will be no mere shadowy, gauzy existence, but a tangible and bodily reality. There will be the warm embrace of friendship, and the real song of praise performed through material organs, giving utterance to the ardent devotions of sinless souls. Eye will sparkle to eye, and heart will beat to heart, and hand will be joined in hand, amid the assemblies and communings of the just in that better land and purer state.

The bearings of this subject upon the future rewards, blessedness, and employments of the heavenly state will be more fully illustrated in the chapter on the nature of Future Happiness, to which the reader is referred, and which should be read in immediate connection with the views presented on the resurrection.

Of the day and hour when this glorious consummation of the Christian's hope will take place, we are not informed. The season is definitely fixed in the purpose of God. Every revolution of earth brings us nearer to it—every breeze wafts us onward, and the shadows of life's closing day, which lie lengthened and cold upon the ground, point eastward to the rising sun. Soon, if prepared, we shall be gathered, with the ransomed, into the paradise above, to await in peaceful rest and hope, and amid the communings of the holy, the dawnings of the long-wished for day. How delightfully attractive the prospect before us! How adapted to cheer and sustain, amid the sorrows and trials of the present state:

"This life's a dream, an empty show;
But the bright world to which I go
Hath joys substantial and sincere;
When shall I wake and find me there?

Oh glorious hour! Oh bless'd abode!
I shall be near and like my God!
And flesh and sin no more control
The sacred pleasures of the soul.

My flesh shall slumber in the ground
Till the last trumpet's joyful sound!
Then burst the chains, with sweet surprise,
And in my Saviour's image rise."

"For this we say unto you by the word of the Lord, that we which are alive and remain unto the coming of the Lord shall not prevent or go before them that are asleep. For the Lord himself shall descend from heaven with a shout, with the voice of the arch-angel, and with the trump of God; and the dead in Christ shall rise first: then we which are alive and remain shall be caught up together with them in the clouds, to meet the Lord in the air: and so shall we ever be with the Lord. *Wherefore comfort one another with these words.*" 1 *Thess.* 4 : 15–18.

CHAPTER V.

THE DAY OF JUDGMENT.

"The Lord, the Sovereign, sends his summons forth,
Calls the south nations and awakes the north;
From east to west the sounding orders spread,
Through distant worlds, and regions of the dead:
No more shall atheists mock his long delay;
His vengeance sleeps no more: behold the day!"

THE world to come, like the present, has its terrors as well as its attractions. Were there nothing in the future but joyous hope, the life to come would be wholly unlike anything which we now know of the government of God.

In our natures, formed there by the Creator, are two great principles, *hope and fear;* to which all motives are addressed, and through which their power is exerted to form our characters and control our actions. It was clearly the design of our Maker that we should be influenced by one desire of happiness, enkindling ever-smiling hope, to seek for the highest good; and that we should be moved by our fear of misery to turn from sin, and shun evil in all its forms. It is in vain for any to say that fear is a low, base, and unworthy passion, and that they will not be influenced by it; for no wise or rational man can help "being moved by fear," to protect himself and his from danger, when he sees it impending. In all the concerns of life, in all the precautions to avoid losses and injuries, and in all the means employed for protection against villanies, and diseases, and death, we see all men who are not utterly reckless and presumptuous, moved continually by fear. It is right. It should be so. We should pervert and deny our natures, and act irrationally, did we not fear as well as hope.

As hope and fear then are a necessary part of our being in the present world, why should they not be in respect to the world to come? If the future life is only a continuation of the present, as the Scriptures teach, must not hope and fear be brought into exercise when eternal things are contemplated? Accordingly we find in Scripture, in the revelations of the world to come, scenes and objects of terror, as well as those trancendently attractive. Those who would blot out all fears from the records of another life, would make a world unsuited to our natures, and contrary to the analogy of all that we see in the world around us. The Scriptures are more in harmony with our natures, and with all the Creator's plans, so far as they are developed to our comprehension.

Among the objects adapted to excite our fears in a future world, is the day of judgment, when the living and the dead will be called to account, and rewarded according to the deeds done in the body.

Around this day, indeed, cluster the terrors of the Lord, by which men should be persuaded to turn from sin, and pursue that course of life which will shield them effectually from all condemnation in the trying hour.

But the day of judgment is not one of unmixed terror, and hence of repulsion to human minds. It has its attractions, great, glorious, and joyous, as will be shown, and will issue in results which will fill a holy universe with joy, and swell the Allelu-ias of the pure forever.

A SOLEMN REALITY.

The following passages prove most conclusively the reality of such a day as revealed in Scripture:

Matt. 10 : 15, "Verily, I say unto you, It shall be more tolerable for the land of Sodom and Gomorrah, in the day of judgment, than for that city." 11 : 24, "But I say unto you, that it shall be more tolerable for the land of Sodom *in the day* of judgment than for thee."

Acts, 17 : 31, "But now God commandeth all men everywhere to repent: Because he hath ap-pointed a day, in the which he will judge the world in righteousness, by that man whom he hath or-dained: whereof he hath given assurance unto all men, in that he hath raised him from the dead." Acts, 10 : 42, "And he commanded us to preach unto the people, and to testify that it is he which was ordained of God to be the judge of quick and dead."

Rom. 2 : 6, 16, "Who will render to every man according to his deeds: in the day when God shall judge the secrets of men by Jesus Christ, according to my gospel." 14 : 10, 12, "But why dost thou judge thy brother? or why dost thou set at naught thy brother? for *we shall all stand* before the judgment-seat of Christ. So then every one of us shall give account of himself to God."

2 *Peter*, 2 : 9, "The Lord knoweth how to deliver the ungodly out of temptations, and to reserve the unjust unto the day of judgment to be punished." 3 : 7, "But the heavens and the earth, which are now, by the same word are kept in store, reserved unto fire against the *day of judgment* and perdition of ungodly men."

1 *John*, 4 : 17, "Herein is our love made perfect, that we may have boldness in the day of judgment: because as he is, so are we in this world."

2 *Cor.* 5 : 10, "For we must all appear before the judgment-seat of Christ; that every one may receive the things done in his body, according to that he hath done, whether it be good or bad."

2 *Tim.* 4 : 1, "I charge thee, therefore, before God, and the Lord Jesus Christ, who shall *judge the quick*, or living, and the dead at his appearing and kingdom." 4 : 8, "Henceforth there is laid up for me a crown of righteousness, which the Lord, the righteous judge, shall give me *at that day*, and not to me only, but unto all them also that love his appearing."

Rev. 20: 12, 13, "I saw the dead, small and great, stand before God; and the books were opened: and another book was opened which is the Book of Life: and the dead were judged out of those things which were written in the books, according to their works. And the sea gave up the dead which were in it; and death and hell delivered up the dead which were in them: and they were judged every man according to their works."

Matt. 12 : 36, "But I say unto you, that every idle word that men shall speak, they shall give account thereof in the day of judgment."

Ecc. 12 : 13, 14, "Let us hear the conclusion of the whole matter: Fear God, and keep his commandments: for this is the whole duty of man. For God shall bring every work into judgment, with every secret thing, whether it be good or whether it be evil."

Jer. 17 : 10, "I the Lord search the heart, I try the veins, even to give every man according to his ways, and according to the fruit of his doings."

It is impossible for us to conceive, how God could reveal in human language, the reality of a future day or time of judgment, more definitely or clearly than it is in these Scriptures.

But these passages not only prove the reality of a day of judgment, but they teach some great and prominent things respecting it, which are worthy of special notice, and which are necessary to perceive its great intent and bearing upon the government of God.

WHEN IT WILL TAKE PLACE.

The time *when* it is to take place is stated. This is not at death—not at the time that each one enters the world of spirits; but *after the resurrection*—when all the living and the dead shall stand before the judgment-seat—when the sea shall give up the dead which are in it, and death and hades, or the invisible world, shall give up the dead which are in them. It shall occur at a time when the inhabitants of ancient Sodom and Gomorrah, and of Tyre and Sidon, and of Nineveh, shall be summoned to appear with the inhabitants of Capernaum, of Chorazan, and Bethsaida. As shown in the chapter on the intermediate state, men will not be prepared for judgment before the resurrection.

THE LENGTH OF TIME INCLUDED.

They teach that every individual of the human race who has lived prior to that time shall appear at the judgment. So affirms the Apostle. For *we must all appear* at the judgment-seat of Christ. So then *every one of us shall* give account of himself to God.

Should the righteous appear first, and be judged, according to Millenarian views, and then the wicked, in their time and order, it would not contradict the general statement that all must appear on that great day, and receive according to the deeds done in the body. Nothing which is here affirmed is impossible. There will be time enough, doubtless, at the judgment, to accomplish all that is predicted will be done on that great day. For the day of judgment, we apprehend, denotes not a period of twelve, or twenty-four hours, but a period of time long enough in which to accomplish all that God has said he will do. The Scriptures justify such a conclusion, and it is rendered necessary by the series and magnitude of events which are to pass in review on that *great* day of God Almighty.

The children of Israel were in the wilderness forty years, and yet the Apostle calls this whole period a day. "The day of temptation in the wilderness." *Heb.* 3: 7–9.

Our Lord said, "I must work the works of him that sent me, while it is day: the night cometh when no man can work." *John*, 9: 4. Here the period of human life, however long or short, is denominated a day.

In the prophets the time during which God in his providence visits a nation for its sins, is termed a day—the day of his wrath. See *Isa.* 63: 4. *Nahum*, 1: 7. *Ez.* 7: 7. The passages are very numerous in which the word day is used to denote a term of trouble or blessing, without limiting the duration. No violence, then, is done to Scripture, when the day of judgment is understood to represent a period of time sufficiently long to accomplish all that God has said he will do, in calling every one to an account, and in bringing every work into judgment with every secret thing, whether it be good or bad.

There seems to be a necessity in the nature of the case, that the day of judgment should occupy a long period of time, perhaps hundreds or thousands of our years. For, if we must all appear before the judgment-seat of Christ, and each one, of all who have ever lived, or shall live, give an account of himself, with every work and secret thing, the time occupied must vastly exceed one brief revolution of earth upon its axis. Let no one be startled at such a statement. *God is never in a hurry.* He takes all the time he needs to accomplish his purposes in the best and most impressive manner, according to the counsels of his own will. He has lived an eternity already, and onward there stretches a series of endless years to come, in which to do all that his soul desires. There will be time enough, then, for all the scenes of the judgment to pass in regular succession, order, and grandeur. Though men are now in such haste in the pursuits of earth, that but few pause to consider their latter end, God will give them time for reflection in the future, and bring up all things in the past in review before them.

This extended view of the judgment now taken, comports more perfectly with the solemnities and unmeasurable interests which cluster around that great day, than does the idea that the eternal destinies of born and unborn millions with the account they are to render, are to be crowded into a few short hours of one short day. Doubtless God could, if he chose, bring each individual's life in review before him in an instant of time, and pronounce an infallibly just verdict in each case, without bringing each one to trial; but such a procedure could in no way so clearly exhibit the justice, equity, and mercy of his decisions to the understanding of finite intelligences, as would the development of each individual case, as described in Scripture. And as the judgment day is not for the benefit of God, but the instruction and conviction of his creatures, may not the Great Judge take time enough to spread out before a finite universe, the grounds of his judgments, and the mysteries of his providence, so as to produce an effect most impressive and instructive upon all who shall be spectators of the scene.

ITS GREAT DESIGN.

The Scriptures above quoted, to prove the reality of a day of judgment, also set forth most clearly and definitely its great design. For we must all appear before the judgment-seat of Christ, that *every one may receive the things done in his body*, or while in his body, according to that he hath done, whether it be good or bad. In many passages of Scripture we are assured that the great law or principle, according to which God will deal with men in the future, will be, to render to every one according to his works. We cannot conceive of a more perfect principle of equity than this. To deal with men according to any other law, would be most manifestly unjust and repulsive to that moral sense implanted in the bosom of every man. A human government is perfect and just only, in proportion as it is based upon this principle of the goverment of God. God is perfect. Justice and judgment are the habitation of his throne; and, therefore, this fundamental law of equity must and will be carried out in the developments of his plans. Hence, a day or time of universal judgment is appointed, the grand design of which is to carry out perfectly, impartially, and eternally this great law.

It is clearly seen that, in the present world, men are not rewarded according to their works. Everything here *seems* to be in disorder. The wicked are prospered, and the righteous are afflicted. Over the impious, judgment lingers, and damnation slumbers; while the virtuous are often crushed beneath the oppressors tread, and pine in solitude; while the vile of earth go unwhipt of justice. And there is an obvious cause for this, clearly and prominently brought to view in Scripture, under the present economy of mercy and probation. Should God so order events, as to render to every man according to his deeds, immediately on the commission of crime, there would be no mercy shown to the sinner, and no system of grace or probation introduced in respect to him. God could not then be long suffering and patient with transgressors. He could not bear with them from generation to generation, and warn, and entreat, and persuade them to turn from their evil ways and live, as he now does in the Gospel of his Son. He bears long, that he may give space for repentance; and he subjects the good to great trials of affliction, that he may discipline and prepare them for their future reward.

Now, he could not thus bear with men, and preserve them through life in a state of grace, mercy, and trial, were he to render to them according to their desert as they went along. The present *apparently* disordered state of things in our world is necessary, under a dispensation of grace and probation, and grows necessarily out of the economy of love, under which we live in connection with the gospel.

It is not strange, therefore, that in consequence of the mercy of God now offered to men, and his long-suffering towards the wicked, and his course of discipline with the good, there should *seem* to be no equity or justice in the administrations of providence. But the revelations of the world to come, and the announcement of a day of judgment, explain the mystery. God now waits to be gracious. But this apparently disordered course of things will not always continue. Though judgment now lingers, a day of reckoning will come when every one will receive according to his deeds. Then God will rectify the disorders of earth, and make a visible and glorious manifestation of his truth, justice, and mercy before the universe.

WHY NECESSARY.

But to some, such a procedure as has been contemplated, in respect to the judgment, may still seem wholly unnecessary. But let it be borne in mind, that it is not maintained, nor is it ever taught in Scripture, that a day of judgment is in any sense necessary for God, to make him acquainted with the characters of men, or to enable him to form a correct and just decision in regard to each individual of mankind. All things are naked and open unto the eyes of him with whom we have to do. With every character—with every secret thing—and with the personal deserts of every creature, he will be as well acquainted before as after the judgment, and, therefore, as well qualified to render an impartial verdict in each case.

But not so with his creatures—the subjects of his universal government. Some definite and detailed manifestation of the grounds of his decisions will be necessary for them, to enable them to comprehend the ways of God, and cordially to approve his government. The Scriptures clearly teach that the Creator has respect to his creatures, and consults their good in what he does. It cannot be disputed that it is both desirable and important that the great principles of his moral government, and the grounds upon which all his decisions are based, should be so exhibited to their understandings, as to call forth their sincere approbation and their cordial submission to all he does.

The righteous have often been exceedingly perplexed in view of the mysteries of providence, as seen in the present world; and they would be equally so in the world to come, were there no developments—no explanations—no revelations made respecting the eternal destinies of men.

When God adjudges the righteous to crowns, and honors and glories in his kingdom, or sentences the wicked to eternal banishment from his presence and the glory of his power, how could all intelligent beings know and understand the justice of God, and the equity of his proceedings, were not the facts upon which the verdict is based, presented to the view of all?

Now, we doubt not, that God intends, in great condescension and mercy to us, to give such an exhibition and illustration of the truth and righteousness of all that he does, as will give us the most unbounded and joyful acquiescence and confidence in his government and character. And how wisely adapted for this purpose will be a judgment day, when all hearts, all secrets, all deeds and all characters shall be revealed in their relation to God, and the destinies assigned.

Suppose, in the case of the wicked, at the judgment, as fact after fact comes out; as the motives and principles by which they have been actuated are disclosed, and their characters are fully and perfectly made known—it shall be shown that they are unfitted for the bliss of heaven—that they have no qualification for the society of the holy, or for that pure service which the sanctified will render to God forever—how will such an exhibition justify the ways of God with the unholy, in excluding them from his presence, and from the heaven of all who love him! for, if they do not love God, and are unlike him and his, in character, and are hence in no way fitted for heaven, will not their exclusion be just and necessary?

And when it is further shown that the wicked have fitted themselves for their doom by wicked works—their obstinate persistence in sin—their refusal to repent—their rejection of the Gospel, and their neglect of all the means appointed of God in love for their salvation—how clearly will his justice appear to all in their condemnation! And how will all this tend to stop the mouth of clamor against the justice and goodness of God, and to reconcile every holy being most perfectly to the decisions of their Maker and Judge!

And how, too, will a revelation of all wickedness at the great day, and all the misery which it has produced under all the varied circumstances in which men have been placed, tend to show the infinite evil of sin, and thus further to justify the severity of God's dealings in respect to transgressions!

Now, we are unable to see how all this could be done in any other way than by a set time—a judgment day; when the decisions of heaven, and the reasons thereof, shall be fully and openly revealed.

We regard, then, a day of judgment, for the purposes assigned in Scripture, as exceedingly desirable, important, and necessary, to unfold the mysteries of providence—to vindicate the character and government of God from all unjust imputations, and suspicions of unkindness, and to confirm the confidence and promote the joy of the universe. We speak not extravagantly, when we affirm that this manifestation and vindication of the character and government of God in respect to his dealings with the righteous and the wicked, will promote the joy of the *universe.* For, it is repeatedly affirmed that the representatives of other orders of beings will be present, and that the attributes of Jehovah developed in the great schemes of his mercy and judgment on earth, are for the instruction of other worlds. The Apostle Paul teaches, *Eph.* 3 : 10, that God does what he does, for the salvation of this world, not simply for us; but "to the intent that now unto principalities and powers in heavenly places," or inhabiting these other worlds in the heavens, "might be known by the church the manifold wisdom of God, according to the eternal purpose which he purposed in Christ Jesus our Lord." The designs of God are vast, wide-circling, and eternal. They are not contracted to earth's narrow limits, but intended for the universal good. We propose to recur to this subject again, when we come to speak of the nature and design of future punishment, and therefore shall not enlarge here. But we must ever bear in mind the universal comprehension of Providence, if we would catch even a glimpse of the glory to be revealed.

ITS ATTRACTIONS TO THE GOOD.

In this connection it will be proper to remark that such a day or time of judgment, as is predicted in the word of God, presents peculiar and joyful attractions to the truly good. Though it will be attended with most solemn and infinite results, they may look forward to it with confidence, and with joy unspeakable and full of glory.

It will be a day in which the mystery of God's providence on earth will be finished. "All the wonderful and perplexing events of providence towards this world will, at this time, be explained to the full conviction of the assembled universe; so that God will appear just when he judges, and clear when he condemns." Then we shall see why tyrants and cruel oppressors have been suffered, for so many long ages, to rule the nations with a rod of iron, and to lord it over the consciences, as well as the bodies of men. Then we shall understand why error and delusion were permitted so generally, and for so long a time, to tread heaven-born truth in the dust, and to lead so many millions blindfolded to ruin.

Then it will appear why the dishonest and seducers, and vile of various name, were suffered, under the eye of a just and sin-hating God, to perfect and carry out their plots of wickedness undisturbed, while the victims of their avarice, lust, and passion mourned uncomforted in secret. Then it will be revealed why the good were compelled to contend with so many difficulties, discouragements and temptations, in their efforts to lead a virtuous and holy life.

Now, must not the prospect of having all these things fully and satisfactorily explained, and all the mysteries of earth finished, be exceedingly pleasant and attractive? What good man has not often felt and said, when dark clouds have hung around the ways of God, and his providences have been involved in inscrutable mystery, I am glad there is a judgment day, when the mystery shall be finished, and the light of eternity be shed upon every dark scene of earth. Who has not sometimes said to himself, when tyrants have raged, and oppressors have triumphed; when he has seen iniquity abounding unrestrained and unrebuked, and when some deep schemes of wickedness have been developed, or so guarded as to be beyond the power of human justice, I rejoice that there is a judgment day coming, when all secret things shall be brought to light, and even-handed justice done to all. As the good on earth always rejoice when justice is administered, and righteousness is ascendant, so will they rejoice in the decisions of the great day. And so when our characters have been assailed, and our motives impugned, and we have been unjustly treated, have we turned our eye to the future, and welcomed a coming judgment.

The day of judgment will be peculiarly attractive to the good, because the government of God will then be fully vindicated, and his character glorified before the universe.

Many have been the complaints which have been made against the government of God by his creatures, and millions have refused to bow in quiet and joyful submission to his will.

The apparent irregularities and inequalities of the present world have led many to deny the existence of a Supreme Ruler, or to question his justice and goodness and wisdom, if he did exist. Against no government or being have more or greater objections ever been made than against God, and especially as revealed in the gospel of his Son. The voice of blasphemy and unbelief and contempt has ascended from generation to generation; and pent up in human hearts have been vast and gloomy mutterings against the Most High. In secret, too, the good have often sighed, and their feet have well nigh slipped, when they have beheld the prosperity of the wicked, and have seen justice linger or languish on earth. In the midst of all these things, believers have often cast their eyes heavenward, and rejoiced in that predicted glorious event, when God will judge the world in righteousness, remedy all disorders, and give to all according to their deeds.

It must be delightful to the good to know that there is a day coming when all disorders will be adjusted—when all inequalities in the administration of justice shall be corrected—when all will receive according to their works, and when the character of that great and holy One, whom they love, shall be vindicated, and rendered infinitely glorious.

On this great day *God will glorify his wisdom.* When the great scheme of his government is revealed, and the great design he proposed to accomplish on earth is made known, and when it is seen how admirably adapted were all the arrangements of providence, and the dispensations of his mercy among men to fulfil his great purposes in the highest welfare of his universe, his wisdom will conspicuously appear; and to the *only wise God,* and our Saviour, will all ascriptions of praise be given.

On this great day, *he will glorify his unspeakable love.* When all secret things are revealed, and truth beams forth as an unclouded sun, it will be seen that all the apparent irregularities of earth, the afflictions of the righteous, and the long suffering manifested toward the wicked amid their prosperity and sin, were only the necessary outgoings of unbounded benevolence. He caused justice to linger, and judgment to slumber, that he might have mercy. He was not slack concerning his promises, but was long-suffering to men, not willing that any should perish, but that all should come to repentance. He sought by goodness and severity mingled, by adversity and prosperity, and by hopes and fears alternately blended, to lead men from sin, and to turn them to himself. And the good, too, he chastised, not in wrath, but in paternal kindness, that he might make them partakers of his holiness. Oh how clearly it will appear at the revelations of the great day, that *God is love*, and that however much overlooked, and slighted, and abused, *this* has been the presiding principle, wide working through the universal frame, and seeking the highest good of all in subordination to the laws of purity, of obedience and universal well being.

On this great day *God will glorify his justice.* When the great trial of human life is summed up, and each one receives according to the deeds done while in the body, impartial justice, the attendant of love, will be magnified. When all the methods which God has taken to save the wicked from sin, are made known, and all the facts in their history come out, and their internal love of sin and rejection of the gospel, it will be shown, beyond denial to all, that sinners have destroyed themselves, and have fitted themselves for misery by their own wicked works, and characters self-formed to evil. It will then be understood by all that the ground of their exclusion from heaven, and the reason why they are sent away to the world of hell, by themselves, is not that God is unkind or unjust, but because they have no likeness to heaven, and are unfitted for it. Love to the good, and justice to the guilty, will require their everlasting punishment from his presence. And so thoroughly will be the conviction of the justice of God in all that is done, that we are assured every mouth will be stopped, and all the world become guilty before God. And the hosts of heaven will sing, "Great and marvellous are thy works, Lord God Almighty; just and true are thy ways, thou King of saints. Who will not fear thee, O Lord, and glorify thy name? for thou only art holy."

It is clear, from the revelations of Scripture respecting the day of judgment, that the character and government of God, in every aspect, will then be vindicated, and placed in a true attitude before an assembled universe. To the good, therefore, the prospect of such a day must be exceedingly attractive and joyous. In proportion as they sincerely love God, and desire the welfare of his government, ought they to rejoice in the bright and eternally glorious prospects which cluster around the great day.

THE TIME OF REWARD TO THE RIGHTEOUS.

But to the redeemed the day of judgment will be pre-eminently attractive—because it will be the set time appointed for them to receive their crowns of glory, and the peculiar rewards promised them, for which they have been long waiting. It will be to the righteous a day of unspeakable joy and triumph. It will be the commencement of a new dispensation, and a higher development of glory than before enjoyed. When the Judge shall publicly recognize them as his friends, and say, "Come, ye blessed of my Father, inherit the kingdom prepared for you from the foundation of the world," or "Well done, good and faithful servant, enter thou into the joy of thy Lord," how will it swell their bosoms with joy unutterable, and full of glory. And yet all this will be at the day of judgment. The Saviour said, "Rejoice, and be exceeding glad; for, great is your reward in heaven," and yet this reward will be given at that day. Can it be otherwise, then, than attractive? As our hearts are drawn upward and onward to the world to come, how clearly does every guide-board along heaven's highway, point us to the judgment-seat, as the place whither we are to go to look for our exceeding great reward.

"How long, dear Saviour, O how long
Shall that bright hour delay?
Fly swiftly round, ye wheels of time,
And bring the wished for day."

TO WHOM IT WILL NOT BE ATTRACTIVE.

The only persons for whom the day of judgment will have no attractions, will be the enemies of God —those who have not loved him, nor obeyed his gospel. To such it must necessarily be a day of fearful terrors. Of this they are faithfully warned in Scripture, that they may be persuaded to repent, and seek a character which shall prepare them for happiness. It will be the day when they must meet him whom they have rejected or neglected, and answer for all the deeds done in the body. It will be the time when all their secret deeds, and secret thoughts and motives, of which they are now ashamed, shall be disclosed, and when they shall receive their last irrevocable sentence, "Depart from me ye cursed." It will be the time when despair, and remorse, and sin, will assert their dark and dismal supremacy over depraved and ruined minds.

It is often said that the destinies of men are dependent on the decisions of the great day. But this is not strictly true. The destinies of men in the future world, depend upon their characters formed here for good or evil. It will be a solemn and fearful thing for the unreconciled to meet God in judgment; but if men would look at the subject aright, it is an equally solemn and fearful thing to live in a world like the present, upon which depend issues so momentous and eternal. There is vastly more at issue, in the characters we form in life, and the course of obedience or disobedience to God which we now pursue, than there will be at the judgment-day. The judgment of the great day, will only be a review of the past—a summoning up of the results of life, and a verdict of acquittal or condemnation based upon an obedience or disobedience to the laws and gospel of God. While, therefore, it will be fearful and solemn to meet the grand results of our doings on earth, it is, if anything, a more serious matter to be treasuring up those results, and every day we live, performing deeds, and forming characters, which are to decide and fix our destinies for life or death.

While we look forward, therefore, to the final decision in our case, and to the fearful or joyful consequences which may follow, we should remember, that whatever of attraction or terror there may be *to us*, in the day of judgment,

> "Time is the season fair of living well,
> The path of glory or the path of hell."

Everything depends on the character now formed, and on the affections now cherished and cultivated. There will be no terrors in the judgment except those which arise from conscious sin and depravity. There will be a full and perfect conviction of sin at the judgment day, which will produce alarm and terror. To produce these convictions will be one great design. Thus it is written, "And Enoch also, the seventh from Adam, prophesied of these, saying, Behold, the Lord cometh with ten thousand of his saints, to execute judgment upon all, and to *convince* all that are ungodly among them of all their ungodly deeds which they have ungodly committed, and of all their hard speeches which ungodly sinners have spoken against him."—*Jude*, 14. Upon these convictions will be based the sentence of the Judge; but it will all depend on what we are, and what we are doing now.

It will be terrible to hear those fearful words, "Depart from me ye workers of iniquity;" but they will be a necessary consequence of sin cherished and committed in life. To the guilty and unsanctified, then only will the judgment day be terrible. And all this may be avoided. "Beloved, *if our heart condemn us not*, then have we confidence toward God."

"Herein is our love made perfect, that we may have boldness in the day of judgment; because as he is, so are we in this world. There is no fear in love; but perfect love casteth out fear: because fear hath torment."—1 *John*, 4 : 17, 18. If, then, we would escape from all fearful apprehensions, and be able to rejoice with the good, there is but one course to be pursued,—fear or love God and keep his commandments; for this is the whole duty of man.

THE PLACE OF JUDGMENT.

It is a matter of no practical importance to us, to know where the scenes of the judgment will be laid, whether on earth, in the air, or in some distant world. But yet it is an inquiry which interests some. From the representations of Scripture, there is reason to infer that the place of judgment will be the earth, and the region of the air around it. At this great day, the Judge will descend to earth. "When Jesus ascended on high, the angels said, Ye men of Galilee, why stand ye gazing up into heaven; for that same Jesus whom ye have seen go up into heaven, shall so come in like manner as ye have seen him go. And in accordance with this, it is written, Behold, he cometh with clouds; and every eye shall see him, and they also which pierced him: and all the kindreds of the earth shall wail because of him." "For the Lord shall descend from heaven with a shout, with the voice of the archangel, and the trump of God—and the dead in Christ shall arise first: then we which are alive and remain, shall be caught up together with them in the clouds, to meet the Lord in the air"—that is, the righteous will be caught up—the wicked will remain upon the earth. These and similar Scriptures imply that the earth itself, and the surrounding air, will constitute the place of Divine manifestation and judgment. It will, no doubt, be a scene transcendently grand and imposing, and well adapted to impress a universe with the majesty and august nature of the scene. The Lord himself will be revealed in flaming fire. Perhaps by this is meant, that he will come down amid some such lightnings and thundering, the insignia of Divine majesty and power, as were displayed on Sinai of old. The judgment will be accompanied or followed by the conflagration of the earth, by which is denoted, not annihilation, but such a geological transformation, as will convert our world and its atmosphere, into a new heaven and earth, in which righteous people only shall ever after dwell.—2 *Pet.* 3 : 13.

It is predicted by the Apostle Peter that increasing numbers, as the day draws on, will disbelieve, contemn, and openly deride all these things. Knowing this first, he says, "That there shall come in the last days scoffers, walking after their own lusts, and saying, 'Where is the promise of his coming? for since the father's fell asleep, all things continue as they were from the beginning of creation.'"

They draw an argument from the stability and

uniformity of the laws of nature, against any such destruction and change in respect to the order and history of our earth as is predicted, in connection with the second glorious appearing of Jesus Christ. But the apostle denies their premises, and affirms that there is no such stability indicated, as to show that our world will roll on, just as it is now, forever. There have been already vast destructions, which have swept over the earth, producing radical changes in its formations and productions. This is revealed not only in Scripture, but confirmed by geological research.

The apostle says, "For this they willingly are ignorant of, that by the word of God the heavens were of old, and the earth standing out of the water and in the water: whereby the world that then was, being overflowed with water, perished: but the heavens and the earth, which are now, by the same word are kept in store, reserved unto fire against the day of judgment and perdition of ungodly men. But, beloved, be not ignorant of this one thing, that one day is with the Lord as a thousand years, and a thousand years as one day. The Lord is not slack concerning his promises, as some men count slackness; but is long-suffering to us-ward, not willing that any should perish, but that all should come to repentance. But the day of the Lord will come as a thief in the night; in the which the heavens (or the atmosphere shall rush) shall pass with a great noise, and the elements shall melt with fervent heat, the earth, also, and the works that are therein shall be burned. Seeing, then, that all these things shall be dissolved, what manner of persons ought ye to be in all holy conversation and godliness, looking for and hasting unto the coming of the day of God, wherein the heavens (or the atmosphere being filled, perhaps, with electrical agents) being on fire, shall be dissolved, and the elements shall melt with fervent heat. Nevertheless we, according to his promise, (See *Is.* 65 : 19–25,) look for new heavens and a new earth, wherein dwelleth righteousness. Wherefore, beloved, seeing that ye look for such things, be diligent that ye may be found of him in peace, without spot, and blameless."

CHAPTER VI.

THE NATURE OF FUTURE HAPPINESS.

"O ye blest scenes of permanent delight!
Full above measure! lasting beyond bound!
A perpetuity of bliss is bliss,
Could you so rich in rapture fear an end,
That ghastly thought would drink up all your joy,
And quite unparadise the realms of light.
Safe are you lodged above these rolling spheres;
The baleful influence of whose giddy dance
Sheds sad vicissitude on all beneath."—YOUNG.

IF presumption may not innocently seek to penetrate beyond the bounds which God has set to light—if curiosity may not, unbidden, try to look into the secrets of eternal love, and if imagination may not substitute her own creations for those substantial glories and sources of unfading happiness, eternal in the heavens, it is surely right—yea, it is our duty to give the most earnest heed to all that is revealed. We may not only look at the more full disclosures of that "far more exceeding and eternal weight of glory" in reserve, but we may gaze in wonder and delight at every ray of light which beams upon us through the opening heavens of truth. We may pause and ponder upon every intimation of things unseen; and as God has given us minds capable of reasoning upon his works and word, and thence drawing conclusions in harmony with truth, we may innocently reason from that which is revealed and seen, to that which is unseen and unwritten, while we are careful that all our deductions are in harmony with the word of God.

If, like the skilful botanist, we diligently gather up the flowers of truth, as they bloom and wave over the sunny field of revelation, and combine them into system, we shall find that a scheme of eternal blessedness is made known to man capable of enrapturing the holy soul, and drawing the pious heavenward with a power which no earthly attractions can weaken or effectually retard.

A PURE MIND ESSENTIAL.

In forming a correct estimate of the nature of future happiness as revealed, it is essential that we first attentively consider the moral character which is fundamental to heavenly enjoyment; for, although, as will be shown, heaven is a *place*, as well as a state of blessedness—a place beautiful and grand beyond conception; and although there will undoubtedly be vast sources of enjoyment, external to ourselves, spread over innumerable worlds, and over eternal ages; yet there must be in us, first, a mind receptive of such pleasures as God will provide—a character corresponding to the works, perfections, and government of the Eternal, or we might be most miserable amid the brightest displays of infinite love.

We know even now that no place however beautiful, or external circumstances however favorable, can make us happy if our minds or moral feelings are not attuned to, and in harmony with the enjoyment they are adapted to bestow. The rich man rolling in affluence, and "clothed in purple and fine linen," and surrounded by all that can regale the senses, or minister to his gratification, may be more miserable at heart, than the poor beggar who solicits the crumbs which fall from his table. Mordecai, who sat next the proud monarch of Assyria, and enjoyed the honors and emoluments of a great and splendid kingdom, was wretched amid all his pomp and glory—a victim of envy and haughty pride.

According to a law of our nature, everything takes the hue of our minds. If we are sad and gloomy, no external beauties—no pleasing landscapes or blooming flowers, can seem cheerful or attractive. If we are proud and jealous, and enviously aspiring, possess what we may, nothing will give us pleasure which does not bow and bend to our wills and caprices. To the man whose soul loatheth food, the most tempting dish would present no prospect of gratification; and to him who has no ear or taste for music, the most enchanting and harmonious strains would be a weariness.

Men often associate happiness with place and circumstances; but all experience, in harmony with Scripture, testifies that a guilty mind cannot be really or permanently happy anywhere; and especially could it not be happy amid the society and the scenes of purity. Even in some holy and happy heaven, resplendent with Jehovah's presence and glory, a mind not reconciled to God in all things, and not at peace with all around, would be miserable, and everything there, as here, would take the hue of his own guilty and unsanctified nature.

Such are clearly the teachings of Scripture; and hence in the very front-ground of all their delineations of future blessedness, is placed a pure heart and a holy character. There must be an entire and joyful reconciliation to God in all things, submission to his laws, and an affectionate relationship to all his creatures, or no place—no external glory, or visions of the blessedness of God, would make us joyous.

Let us, then, carefully look over the essential elements of that character, which God in his word requires to fit us for the exceeding great and blissful rewards to be bestowed.

LOVE AN ELEMENT.

Among all the qualifications necessary to prepare us for happiness in any world, or sphere of being, love is pre-eminent. It is the great and fundamental principle of the law of God, in this or any other world. It is the fulfilling of the law, and comprehends in substance all that is enjoined in Scripture. To God, it must be supreme; to all creatures, subordinate and perfect. Now, it is easy to see how this love, going forth supremely and continually in active exercise towards God, and comprehending in its wide and warm embrace, all intelligent beings, with an affection as sincere and ardent as that which seeks its own good, will lay the foundation of true and substantial bliss, and make each one the promoter as well as the recipient of happiness.

Though it may not now be known what kind offices there may be for any one to perform in the world to come—what good there may be to be done among the ransomed above, yet we know that this perfect love to God and man will unite all hearts as one, and gather them harmoniously around the throne of Jehovah, to pay their homage and devotion, and will prepare them to rejoice in others good, and to perform any service God may require or circumstances demand.

Love, then, must be an essential element in any character destined for a holy and happy heaven. The command which enjoins it, came from the overflowings of the benevolence of the infinite Mind. God has not more regard for his own honor and happiness, in demanding as his right this supreme affection, than he has for the highest welfare of man. It is impossible to conceive how even almighty power could prepare men for a world of perfect blessedness, in any other way than through the medium of universal love; for where love is wanting, there must be alienation, variance, hatred, and every evil work. Hence, God, in great kindness and earnestness, is now seeking in the Gospel of his Son—in the renewings of his Spirit, and by the power of his truth, and all the influences and agencies by which we are surrounded, to beget within us and train us to undying love.

But love stands not alone. It is not a mere passive virtue, inactive and unproductive. It bears fruit unto eternal life, and gathers around it an assemblage of virtues, dependent on it, beautiful and symmetrical. It is to the moral, what the heart is to the physical system—its very life. Its pulsations are felt through all the body. It gives vigor and character to every other virtue of which it is possible to conceive, and is hence greater than all; but it exists not alone, for in the character to which heaven is promised—

RIGHTEOUSNESS IS AN ELEMENT.

"Without holiness no man shall see the Lord." This is composed of justice and truth, combined with love, and flowing from it, as naturally and necessarily as a stream from an overflowing fountain. No man can love God supremely, and not render to him the homage and obedience due to his name; and no one can love his neighbor as himself, and not act truthfully and righteously in all things respecting him. There would manifestly be no peace and happiness without this rectitude of character flowing from and assimilated to love. What better, morally, could heaven be than earth, were injustice and deceit to enter? Were such admitted to the inner gates of Paradise, how would the selfish passions still prevail—pride, envy, intrigue, and hate? and how, like laws of repulsion, would they drive asunder, and scatter to destruction all the elements of good! God has, therefore, purposed and revealed that this shall never be. In the fifteenth Psalm, this question is definitely asked and answered —"*Lord, who shall abide in thy tabernacle? Who shall dwell in thy holy hill?*" *Answer*—"He that walketh uprightly, and worketh righteousness, and speaketh the truth in his heart. He that backbiteth not with his tongue, nor doeth evil to his neighbor, nor taketh up a reproach against his neighbor. In whose eyes a vile person is contemned; but he knoweth them that fear the Lord. He that sweareth to his own hurt, and changeth not. He that putteth not out his money to usury, nor taketh a reward against the innocent. He that doeth these things shall never be moved."

It is seen here that perfect rectitude and truthfulness of character are required to give admission to the dwelling-place of Jehovah, and to prepare those who enter for its enjoyment. What then will the dishonest, the liar, and the impious do? Into what place, or sphere, will they enter? The harmonies of heaven, and the peaceful purity of its inmates, would be interrupted and despoiled, were they admitted. Do such turn to the gospel, and rejoice in the free and unmerited salvation which its abounding mercy and grace reveal? But the gospel does not contradict the law, or lower the standard of Scriptural perfection. It says—

"For the grace of God that bringeth salvation hath appeared to all men, teaching us that denying ungodliness, and worldly lusts, we should live soberly, righteously, and godly in this present world; looking for that blessed hope, even the glorious appearing of the great God, and our Saviour Jesus Christ; who gave himself for us that he might redeem us from all iniquity and purify unto himself a peculiar people zealous of good works." *Titus*, 2: 11.

Wherever we look, then, to the Old or New Testament, to the la or to the gospel, we find the same general rectitude of character described as essential to give admission to the kingdom of God. How, then, can the unrighteous hope for the bliss of heaven, who have no hungerings and thirstings after holiness? "Know ye not that such cannot inherit the kingdom of God?" 1 *Cor.* 6: 9.

But this is not all. Set around that perfect rectitude of character to which love gives birth, is a constellation of graces, presented in Scripture, which give dignity to perfection, and shed a halo of unfading beauty and glory around the pathway of the just.

HUMILITY AN ELEMENT.

Next to love, among the most prominent and beautiful of the Christian graces is humility. This is a virtue peculiarly dear to God. "For, thus saith the high and lofty One that inhabiteth eternity, whose name is holy: I dwell in the high and holy place, with him also that is of a *contrite* and *humble* spirit, to revive the spirit of the *humble,* and to revive the heart of the contrite ones." *Is.* 57: 15. "But he giveth more grace. Wherefore he saith, God resisteth the proud, but giveth grace unto the humble." *James,* 4: 6.

Humility is the opposite of pride, and arrogance, and self-exaltation. It is that which leads us to take low views of ourselves, to esteem others, in respect to preferment and office, better or before ourselves, which renders us happily submissive to the Divine will, and content with God's allotments, whatever they may be.

Where it exists in perfection, there can be no envy or jealousy, when others are exalted above us, or in preference to us, or suspicion that we are esteemed less than we deserve. There can be no boasting, or selfish ambition, or haughtiness, when we are more favored than some, or any other feeling which brings us in heart or interest in collision with another.

And how essential will all this be to perfect order and happiness in a world of joy. With this grace in full and joyous exercise, each individual will cheerfully take the place for which the faculties and powers given him, fit him, and which heaven appoints, and will lead him to rejoice in others' good in preference to his own, and they in his, in return.

If humble in heaven, we shall not envy Gabriel's exaltation; nor will he look down from the dazzling heights he occupies on the meanest creature with haughtiness or contempt. If Paul has a brighter crown of glory than some, and shall shine as a star more brilliant than others, we shall not love him the less, but shall think any place beneath the smiles of the Holy One good enough for those so unworthy.

And thus what love, what order, what harmony, what rejoicings, mutual and eternal, will be produced? O what a world will that be, where perfect humility, springing from perfect love, shall shed its mild and peaceful, and subduing, and attractive influence over all? Can there be a heaven without humility? Can we be truly happy now, or anywhere without it? "He that humbleth himself shall be exalted, yea, exalted to heaven; but he that exalteth himself shall be abased.

FAITH AN ELEMENT.

It is a common sentiment that in the world to come, "faith will be swallowed up in vision," and hence will be no more called into exercise. Is it so taught in Scripture? It is true that the salvation of our souls, and those things distinctly revealed as objects of faith, will become matters of sense and vision when we are welcomed to heaven by the approving verdict of the Judge of all; but is it ever revealed that faith will cease?

The apostle says, "Now *abideth* faith, hope, charity—these three; but the greatest of these is charity." Love is the greatest, because it gives existence to faith and hope; but faith, as well as it, *abideth*. This passage gives clear intimation and assurance that it will exist and flourish in an immortal life.

It is quite certain that faith will be an essential element in that character which will render heaven blessed, and that the situation of the saints will call it into highest exercise. The redeemed, we may well suppose, will be filled with joy unspeakable, as they stand amid the fruition of the future world, and contemplate in endless perspective the opening vista of the far-reaching future; and the idea that these joys will never terminate, but continue to increase as their powers expand, and their ever-enlarging capacities call for new supplies, must give a permanence and perfection to their happiness exceedingly enrapturing.

But suppose that amid these scenes their faith in the promises and faithfulness of God should fail, and the gloomy thought take possession of their minds, that these bright prospects might soon fade through their own fall, or the instability of the promises and government of God, what indescribable sorrow would a want of faith, under such circumstances, produce?

And now, how can the saints in heaven know that such will not be the sad ending of all their joys? How can they be assured that God will never change? or, if he should not, that they will never sin, and ruin themselves? They know that sin once entered heaven, and cast from their exalted seats the angels who kept not their first estate. Amid the uncorrupted bowers of Eden, too, sin entered, and seduced our first parents from holiness and happiness. With such melancholy examples before them, how can the holy know that a similar fate will not befall them? that, left to their own unaided powers, they may not, in some hour of fierce temptation, fall into condemnation, and be made as miserable as the lost? It was just as improbable and impossible in itself considered, if not more so, that the angels should fall from heaven, and that Adam should sin, before their melancholy defection, as it is that the saints shall forever maintain allegiance and purity in heaven. And as God left them to fall, how do they know but that he will leave them to a similar fate? Can anything but faith in God, and in his word, give them any certain confidence that they will not?

It is certain, in regard to the saved, that they will never sin or perish. But why not? Because God has promised them eternal life. He has said they shall never perish. Their safety, therefore, must depend entirely upon the truth and faithfulness of God; and they can only be assured of the perpetuity of holiness and happiness, by their faith in the immutability of God and his truth. Here, then, their faith, made perfect, must rest with a confidence so strong as to exclude continually every suspicion and doubt.

There will be a necessity for faith then in the world to come, and this with love must *abide.* And the faith there exercised will be of precisely the same kind as that which we now possess, except that it will then be perfect, and all-controlling. Faith then, as now, will be the substance of things hoped for, the evidence of things not seen; for even in heaven there will be stretching out before the redeemed an eternity filled with innumerable objects of beauty and grandeur, unseen and hoped for, to which faith will look, and of which it will be the evidence and substance.

The plans of God will be continually going on through eternal ages, and his purposes will be perpetually developed. How can we be peaceful and happy amid these scenes, in which we must fulfil our part, without a simple and perfect faith in God? We shall certainly need it, while we are dependent on the Infinite, and unable to grasp the whole which the mind of God conceives.

This view of the subject is rendered certain, we judge, from the great prominence given to faith in Scripture as preparatory to heaven, and from the means which God now employs to strengthen in his people this essential grace. The Apostle Peter, in speaking of the great affliction which Christians were called to suffer, says, "Wherein ye greatly rejoice, though now for a season (if need be) ye are in heaviness through manifold temptations: that the trial of your faith, being much more precious than of gold that perisheth, though it be tried with fire, might be found unto praise, and honor, and glory, at the appearing of Jesus Christ."

Here we are informed that one prominent design, in the accumulated trials of life, is to strengthen and purify our faith, that it may be found perfect at the appearing of our Lord. But why this, if faith is to terminate as we enter the world to come? Why should life be spent in cultivating that which is to have no exercise in the better land? It seems clear from the fact that so many means are employed to beget, and strengthen faith in the present world, and that even in the last agonies of death the Redeemer takes so much pains to perfect it, that it will be essential to our future happiness, and will have a high office to fulfil in administering to the permanence and perfection of the glory to be revealed.

That faith then will abide in the future world, and constitute an essential element in that perfected character, which will constitute the basis of all happiness, seems eminently Scriptural, and in full harmony with nature and reason. It tends to give us a more definite and rational view of the world to come, and places before us the most weighty considerations, cheerfully to acquiesce in all those allotments of providence, which are designed to increase and mature faith.

HOPE AN ELEMENT.

If faith "*abideth*," hope must also. Scripture and reason unite in showing that it will constitute an essential element in our future characters and happiness. "It cannot consistently be supposed that the full measure of good in reserve will be bestowed at once, at our first introduction to heaven; but rather that there will be successive developments of truth, and things unseen through unending ages, calling forth new joys, and new songs of thanksgiving, of admiration, and praise, from fresh discoveries and displays of the perfections of God, in his works and ways. Every finite being is capable of accession; and in knowing, and doing, and attaining and enjoying, there will be an infinite progression before us."—*Jay.*

If these things are so, then there must be hope in heaven. There will be a continued and joyous expectation of things to come—hope pluming her bright wings for an upward and an immortal flight, and giving rise to the pleasures of rapturous anticipation. Accordingly, we are assured that Christ hath begotten us again unto a *lively hope*—a hope which will never die. The saints who are now in heaven, are resting in hope of the redemption of their bodies; and when the dawn of the resurrection morn sheds its blushes round the spheres, hope will still look onward to the bright career of eternal ages. In this view of the subject, how pleasing the reflection, that "tribulation, even now, worketh patience; and patience experience, and experience *hope.*" But this is not all.

PATIENCE MUST BE AN ELEMENT.

This must ever accompany hope. "But if we hope for that we see not, then do we with patience wait for it."

Patience as commonly understood, denotes that calm temper of mind which bears evils without murmuring or discontent. Now, as there are to be no evils in heaven, no sighing or suffering, it is manifest that patience in the sense of the endurance of afflictions will not exist. But this is not the only, or chief sense in which the word is used in Scripture.

"Be patient, therefore, brethren" says the apostle James, "unto the coming of the Lord. Behold the husbandman waiteth for the precious fruits of the earth, and hath long patience for it, until he receive the early and the latter rain. Be ye also patient; establish your hearts; for the coming of the Lord draweth nigh."

In the case of the husbandman there is no pain, or sorrow, or affliction implied in that quiet and contented composure with which he waits for the joyful harvest. Having used the appropriate means, and committed the precious seed to the ground, and intrusted the result in the hand of a kind providence, he quietly and contentedly waits until the revolving seasons cause it to bring forth. This quiet, submissive, and joyful waiting for any good which we expect in the future, is patience in the Scriptural sense. And must it not exist hereafter? It has already been shown that hope must and will exist there.

And those expectations to which the opening and brightening prospects of far distant ages will give rise, may be long delayed. It may require myriads of years—cycles of ages which we cannot now compute, to unfold and fully develop to created minds, those schemes of grace and glory which a God of infinite wisdom, power, and love, may devise for the enjoyment of his holy and obedient subjects. And there will be need of patience to render us content and happy under the long delays of God's infinite plans, which will be seen by all to be ordered in wisdom and goodness. No doubt the spirits of just men made perfect, now in heaven, and who are waiting in expectancy the resurrection, and the judgment, and those higher rewards which will then be dispensed, have need of patience, and find it essential to their present contentment and bliss. If there is not patience in heaven, there must be impatience. And could it be a happy world were it so?

If patience is not to exist and be exercised in the world to come, why does the apostle James so earnestly exhort its cultivation? "My brethren, count it all joy when ye fall into divers temptations; knowing this, that the trial of your faith worketh *patience*.

But let patience have her perfect work, that ye may be perfect and entire, wanting nothing." But why should God carry men through divers and fiery trials for the purpose of working patience in them, if it is to have no place or exercise in a better life?

Now, this fact carries irresistable conviction to my own mind, that we shall need patience in perfection to prepare us for heaven.

God himself is a God of patience; Jesus is patient, meek and lowly in mind as he ever was, and so it will be necessary for us to be, to be like him, and enjoy his society and love. And then the high offices we are to fill as kings and priests unto God, may require the exercise of patience in a different sense still from that contemplated. We proceed to consider as elements of our future characters—

SUBMISSION AND RESIGNATION.

As they are now essential to Christian character, so they will be necessary to the harmony and blessedness of the kingdom of God. As they now greatly minister to the peace and contentment of life, so they will be no less fruitful in righteousness, peace, and joy in God amid the wondrous scenes of eternity. Heaven would be as disobedient as earth, and as fruitful of misery as hell, were not all there entirely submissive and resigned to the will of the Supreme. And it is therefore to prepare men for heaven, that God in love and condescension now seeks to bring all into a willing and joyful submission to him, and in all life's afflictions to train us for the skies.

Were it necessary, and did our limits permit, it might be shown that any virtue or grace enjoined in Scripture, is demanded not only for its influence in life, but especially for its influence on the life to come.

"And besides this," says Peter, "giving all diligence, add to your faith virtue; and to virtue, knowledge; and to knowledge, temperance; and to temperance, patience; and to patience, godliness; and to godliness, brotherly kindness; and to brotherly kindness, charity. For if these things be in you and abound, they make you that ye shall neither be barren nor unfruitful in the knowledge of our Lord Jesus Christ. For so an entrance shall be ministered unto you abundantly into the everlasting kingdom of our Lord and Saviour Jesus Christ."

But why should we be so diligent in cultivating these graces, if they are not to have place and power in the everlasting kingdom of Christ?

It is a great, and practical, and mischievous error, that some have taught, that the essential graces of the Christian, required in Scripture, will not be called into exercise in the world to come. Is not the prevalence of this error a reason why so little attention is paid to their cultivation and exercise by the great mass who profess to love the Saviour. O there is reason to fear that many, when weighed at the last, in the balances of eternity, will be found wanting, in all that is essential to fit them for heaven, because they have relied upon a name to live, while they have been dead to those things requisite in every character which is heavenly. The revelations of the Word of God clearly teach us that we shall need just that character, which the combination of these graces, blended as the colors of the rainbow, will form, to enter fully into the joy of our Lord. Such a character possessed by the innumerable hosts of heaven, will be beautifully and sublimely adapted, beneath the smiles of infinite love, and in association with each other, to produce the fruits of eternal fruition. The societies of heaven will be composed of those in whose characters all these graces of the Spirit, portrayed in Scripture, will be blended in delightful harmony and consistency. And hence, all will be prepared cheerfully to take the place which heaven appoints, joyfully to do the work God assigns, and contentedly and happily to mingle and participate in those unfolding purposes, which an eternity may disclose.

NECESSITY OF AN EXTERNAL HEAVEN.

Having now considered the character which, according to Scripture, is required to fit us for association with others, and happiness in any place or sphere, and from which, as a never-failing source, in union with God our blessedness is to flow—we are prepared to turn and view those things external to ourselves, which God has promised, and which will be found to be wisely and perfectly adapted to every faculty, want, and aspiration of a holy mind.

Though the elements of an endless life of happiness must be within us, in the moral states and character of our own minds; yet there must be something real and tangible without us, upon which our minds can act, and towards which our affections can flow, and upon which all our powers can be employed in appropriate and delightful exercise. The eye must have beauties, infinitely diversified, upon which to gaze—the ear must listen to the voices of love, and the melody of sounds, and every other sense must have its appropriate external objects of excitement and pleasure. Love must go forth and answer to love's call in others, and in all respects an aspiring, expanding, and growing mind, must have free room to act itself out, externally, upon and in connection with kindred objects, and must increase in knowledge by unrestrained intercourse with the works and ways of God.

There must, in fact, be an external nature or universe, in all its illimitable expanse, as now seen, with all its infinite diversity of objects, creatures and scenery, to give the holy full employment in the delightful exercise of all their powers.

Shut a good man up in some seclusion, away from the objects of his love, and let his mind have no liberty to range and study amid God's wondrous works, and though he would never feel the goadings of a guilty conscience, his mind would droop as a plant shut out from light, and his powers and graces decay as one buried in the tomb. Simple holiness would not be enough to render him blessed. A holy mind, such as the Scriptures require, is only a preparation for, and an essential element in the happiness to be revealed. It must be placed amid scenes and associations of created beings, and such display of the God of love as will draw out, and give full and indefinite expansion and gratification to all its desires, promptings, aspirings and loves. The "exceeding great and precious promises," given to us in Scripture, refer to things in full harmony with these suggestions.

HEAVEN A PLACE.

As the mind needs a heaven without it as well as within it, God has promised to the good a glorious and happy place, as their peculiar home in another life, and which has a distinct and definite locality somewhere in the universe.

Some maintain that the heaven of Scripture is not a place, but a mere state of happiness, which may exist anywhere.

It is a fundamental part of the spiritual system of Swedenborg, that in another life we are altogether separated from material worlds and things, and that in the spiritual world "there are no spaces or distances," and consequently no localities, "but there are appearances of spaces, and these are according to their states of life, and the states of life according to the states of love."

Now, for one I confess I can form no idea of any world in which there is nothing material, and in which there are no spaces, or distances, or localities, nor can I conceive how things having their own peculiar forms, and existing as distinct persons, can inhabit an immaterial world in which no spaces, localities, or time exist. But such, I am confident, is not the teachings of the word of God. Not a word of any such misty, transcendental moonshine, is to be found in Scripture. My soul longs for something more substantial to feast upon and enjoy than this.

The Scriptures do not enter into any formal argument on the question whether heaven is a mere state, or a place of happiness; but they everywhere speak of it as a place, and designedly employ language which is adapted to convey the idea of a glorious and happy place, where, in a peculiar sense, is the abode of God. Take such passages as the following:

"Rejoice, and be exceeding glad: for great is your reward *in heaven*."

"Take heed that ye despise not one of these little ones; for *in heaven*, I say unto you, *their* angels do always behold the face of my Father *in heaven*."

"Lay up for yourselves treasures *in* heaven."

"In my Father's house are *many mansions*: if it were not so, I would have told you. I go to prepare a *place* for you. And if I go and prepare a *place* for you I will come again and receive you unto myself; that where I am, there ye may be also."

John, 14 : 2, 3. To these, numerous other passages might be added, all of which speak of heaven as a place high and holy.

That heaven is a place, and a material place, too, is further manifest from the fact that our Lord ascended thither in his resurrection body; and wherever he is corporeally, there is heaven. "*Where* I am, *there* shall also my servants be." Enoch and Elijah were translated in their material bodies, and as they are in heaven in these bodies, heaven must be a material place.

The same thing is clearly evinced in the doctrine of the resurrection. As our *vile bodies* are to be raised, changed, and fashioned like unto Christ's glorious body, and we are, therefore, to exist in heaven in a material form, heaven must be a material place. We might argue it, also, from the nature of our minds, and the necessities of the case. Our minds are now manifestly fitted for and adapted to an external world or universe. Constituted as our minds are, how could they grow and expand, except in connection with just such a universe as now blooms and glows with Jehovah's glory, and rolls in grandeur around us? If we are to be the same or similar beings in another life as here, we shall need the same or similar connections with an external world, to call our powers into action, and to manifest to us in living forms, and in infinite and endless variety, the perfections of the Incomprehensible.

Now although, as has been shown, the elements

of heaven must be within us, yet who can say that a glorious outward heaven—a *place* beautiful and grand, and in all respects adapted to the mind in its sanctified state, would not be immensely desirable, and adapted to minister to our enjoyment? The simple bible view of heaven, as a place, as well as a state of happiness, is calculated to give us infinitely more pleasing and definite views of the world to come, and a more tangible realization of future things, than the spiritual theories which make us flit about and dance in empty air, without locality, distance, measurement, or time.

Heaven is described to us, as in a peculiar sense the *Throne* of God—the high and holy place—as a paradise, or garden of delights—as the abode of angels, where they always behold the face of our Father—and as the resting place of the spirits of just men made perfect. No very definite description is given of it in Scripture, and, no doubt, for the best of reasons—that no language could at present convey to our minds a correct idea of its exceeding beauty and glory. From the clear intimations given, we have reasons to infer that it must transcend all human conception. "Many beautiful forms pass before us, as we journey through life, entrancing our senses; and there are in earth, and in the visions of fancy, many images of exquisite loveliness;" but we may well suppose that heaven immeasurably surpasses them all.

"Dreams cannot picture a world so fair,—
Sorrow and death may not enter there;

Time doth not breathe on its fadeless bloom,
'Tis beyond the clouds, and beyond the tomb."

What could be more attractive to the holy, than the idea of such a place.

ITS LOCALITY.

But where is heaven? Suppose we cannot answer, it will not in any way disprove that it is a place, and has locality somewhere amid the innumerable bright orbs that roll above and around us. If we knew exactly where it was, it would be of no essential, practical benefit. It is a mere question of curiosity. We answer, then, we do not know where it is. The supposition of Dick may or may not be true. It is at least harmless, while it is pleasing, and beautiful, and sublimely glorious. It may be the central world of the universe. Science reveals that our sun and its system of planets, is only one of a grand system of suns and worlds, composed of the milky-way. Far-off in the distance, beyond the galaxy, are seen, by the aid of the telescope, other systems as beautiful and resplendent as our own. "It is now considered, by astronomers, as highly probable, if not certain, that all the systems of the universe revolve around one common centre, and that this centre may bear as great a proportion, in point of magnitude, to the universal assemblage of systems as the sun does to his surrounding planets." Now, what more plausible than that this great central universe may be, in a peculiar sense, the throne of Jehovah, around which all else move in grandeur and harmony.

The Saviour said, "In my Father's house are many mansions," and this may be intended to teach us that heaven may be composed of an assemblage of many worlds, each fitted up by the Redeemer, and adapted to the various orders and societies of the good who may fill his house—and between all these there may be the most easy communication and delightful intercourse.

> "Fair, distant land, could mortal eyes
> But half its charms explore,
> How would our spirit long to rise,
> And dwell on earth no more.
> No cloud those distant regions know,
> Realms ever bright and fair!
> For sin, the source of mortal woe,
> Can never enter there."

THE SOCIETY OF HEAVEN.

As the mind, trained and fitted for enjoyment, will need full exercise for every faculty and affection, heaven we are assured will be composed of a glorious assembly or society of associated and kindred minds.

Our natures clearly indicate that society is essential to happiness. We could not exercise love, gratitude, humility, patience, meekness, and the faculty of communication, in any extended sense without it. God made us, and has given us the qualifications for association. "It is not good for men to be alone." "He setteth even the solitary in families." But for society to be a means and source of happiness, it must be congenial. It must be comprised of kindred minds united in affection, interest, and pursuit. The reverse would be misery. An association of uncongenial spirits, with clashing interests and vile affections, would kindle an unquenchable fire of discord and torment. But who compose the society of heaven? The apostle has given us the sum in the twelfth chapter of Hebrews, "But ye are come unto Mount Zion, and unto the city of the living God, the heavenly Jerusalem, and to an innumerable company of angels, —to the general assembly and church of the first-born, which are written in heaven, and to God the Judge of all, and to the spirits of just men made perfect, and to Jesus the Mediator of the new covenant, and to the blood of sprinkling, that speaketh better things than that of Abel."

What an assemblage of glorious persons is here presented! What a society, composed of the choice spirits of the universe. Let us think them over one by one. Conspicuous above all others is *God the Judge of all*—him whom we have been taught to call "Our Father in heaven." In view of the mystery and infinitude of his being, our minds have often been confounded and overwhelmed. His judgments, too deep for human comprehension, have filled us with amazement and awe. His wonderful perfections have humbled and caused us to tremble, while his love mildly beaming through all, has often kindled the most lively and animating hope. And now what will it be to be with him! to see him as he is; to look up and meet the smiles of a Father—to dwell "in his presence, where is fulness of glory, and at his right hand where are pleasures forever more."

And then in association with, and equal to the Father, will be *Jesus the Mediator*, who loved us, and redeemed us unto God by his blood. As Christ is now the brightness of the Father's glory, and the express image of his person, so he will, in a particular sense, constitute the glory and attraction of the society of heaven. The solar system would not lose more of its glories were the sun to be blotted out, than would heaven, were Jesus not there. As he is now the medium through which the love and mercy of God flow down to men, so we are assured that it will be through the Lamb slain, that the blessings of the world to come will be bestowed. "And he said to me, These are they which come out of great tribulation, and have washed their robes, and made them white in the blood of the Lamb. Therefore are they before the throne of God, and serve him day and night in his temple: and he that sitteth on the throne shall dwell among them. They shall hunger no more; neither thirst any more; neither shall the sun light on them, nor any heat." *Why not?* "For the Lamb, which is in the midst of the throne shall feed them, and shall lead them unto living fountains of waters: and God shall wipe away all tears from their eyes."

We see in this passage how the glories of the Father and the Son are united and blended. Jesus is not more the attraction of heaven than the Father. They are one; and their beauties and honors are inseparable. But the Saviour may be most conspicuous, because associated still with our nature, and still the Mediator, through whom the streams of eternal blessedness will flow to all the holy.

Next in order, as a part of the society of heaven, we may contemplate "an innumerable company of angels." These are the sons of God, who have never sinned, and the morning stars who sang together when earth's foundations were laid. They are God's messengers, and the executioners of his will. From Adam down they have humbly and joyfully ministered to men in sorrow, temptation, and danger, and at each successive step have been deeply interested in the unfoldings of salvation.

Now to be in, and a part of the society of such beings, must be exceedingly joyous. Who would not love to see and converse with those guardian angels, who have watched over us and our "little ones"? Who would not love to hear them tell how anxious they were for our welfare, and how they rejoiced when we yielded to God's influence and theirs, and turned from sin to the love and obedience of the gospel.

Then there will be the Heavenly—the New Jerusalem—the spirits of just men made perfect, composing the church of the first-born, whose names are written in heaven. Among them will be the patriarchs and prophets, apostles and martyrs, and the lovely and good of every name, age, and nation.

"I beheld," says John, "and lo, a great multitude which no man could number, of all nations, and kindred, and people, and tongues, stood before the throne, and before the Lamb, clothed with white robes, and palms in their hands; and cried with a loud voice, saying, salvation to our God, which sitteth upon the throne, and unto the Lamb."

We have, then, in the clear revelations of Scripture, the demands of our social natures fully met. External to ourselves, in those mansions Jesus has gone to prepare, will be an assemblage of choice and holy beings, "such as earth saw never," united in love and obedience to God, and bound to each other by ties of tenderest affection. To this society, so congenial and adapted to our purified minds, we shall undoubtedly have constant and pleasing access; and in communion and association with them we shall perform the high and enrapturing services of the sanctuary above. In this society we may certainly expect

GREAT SOCIAL ENJOYMENT.

This point is not distinctly argued in Scripture, but it is incidentally brought to view, and illustrations are given which satisfactorily confirm the position.

Thus it is written, "And I say unto you that many shall come from the east and the west, and shall sit down with Abraham, Isaac, and Jacob, in the kingdom of heaven." *Matt.* 8: 11.

"And ye shall see Abraham, and Isaac, and Jacob, and all the prophets in the kingdom of God. And they shall come from the east and from the west, from the north and from the south, and shall sit down in the kingdom of God." *Luke,* 13: 28, 29.

These passages certainly intimate the most familiar and endeared social enjoyment. What else can be meant by sitting down with patriarchs and prophets in the kingdom of God? reclining with them, as at a table or feast, in intimate association and communion? The idea of a supper or feast anciently, was undoubtedly associated with the most fraternal and pleasant intercourse. And it is difficult to see how the social character of heaven and heavenly enjoyments would be more clearly or touchingly presented than by representing its guests as reclining fraternally at the table of the Lord.

There are other passages of Scripture which bear directly on this point. Our Lord says, "For I say unto you, I will not any more eat thereof, until it be fulfilled in the kingdom of God. For I say unto you, I will not drink of the fruit of the vine, until the kingdom of God shall come. And I appoint unto you a kingdom, as my father hath appointed unto me; that ye may eat and drink at my table in my kingdom." *Luke,* 22: 16, 18, 29, 30.

Now, whatever all this may mean, can it be reasonably doubted that these sayings do teach that there will be great social entertainment and delights in heaven? This is the great idea conveyed under the image of a feast, to which patriarchs, and prophets, and apostles, and all the saved will sit down, and not that the kingdom of God will be one of sensual entertainment.

All this is in entire harmony with the social natures God has given us. The Creator has never formed anything in vain. He intended that every instinct and faculty of our natures should have its appropriate external gratification. Can it be supposed that our social propensities and powers will be blotted out? If not, they must have exercise and pleasure.

Now, how delightfully do all the teachings and intimations of Scripture blend and harmonize with the natures God has given us. And this is a high and convincing proof of their rationality and inspiration. What a field for thought is here opened! O how delightful it will be to spend an hour in conversation with Adam, with Moses, or Gabriel! To hear them tell of their experience, and of their present views and prospects and adoring conceptions of the Lord! And thus in turn, and through the years of an endless life, with all others. How pleasant it will be for those who have been associated in labors and trials on earth, to talk them all over, and to speak of all God's wondrous works of love, and then unite with the great company in some sweeter song "unto Him that loved us, and washed us fron our sins in his own blood." But this is not all, for the Scriptures quoted clearly intimate, that there will be in heaven.

PERSONAL RECOGNITION.

It is affirmed that we shall see Abraham, Isaac, and Jacob, and all the prophets in the kingdom of God; among whom will be Enoch, Noah, Moses, Samuel, Elijah, Elisha, Isaiah, Jeremiah, David, Daniel, Ezekiel, and all others. Now, if we shall see all these, is it not clear that we shall personally recognize and know them? And if these, may we not infer that we shall as certainly see and know all others, and especially those whom we have loved, and walked to the house of God in company with on earth?

The scene which occurred upon the Mount, at the time of Christ's transfiguration, teaches the same thing. It is said, "And behold there talked with him two men, which were Moses and Elias, who appeared in glory, and spoke of his decease, which he should accomplish at Jerusalem." In this scene all who were present are represented as knowing each other. Although Moses and Elias had left the world at periods separated by hundreds of years, yet they had become acquainted in heaven, and now they visited together the Lord of glory.

The apostle Paul distinctly recognized this doctrine. In writing to the Colossians, he says, after referring to Christ as the hope of glory, "Whom we preach, warning every man, and teaching every man in all wisdom; that we may *present every man perfect* in Christ Jesus." From this language, we learn that the apostle was stimulated to be faithful in the discharge of his duties by the anticipated pleasure of meeting his converts in the heavenly world, and presenting them to Christ, as the trophies of the power of a Saviour's love.

In his epistle to the Thessalonians he says, "For what is our hope, or joy, or crown of rejoicing? Are not even ye in the presence of our Lord Jesus Christ, at his coming? For ye are our glory and joy." "The manner in which the apostle speaks, in this passage, shows that he expected to know his converts," in another world. If so, we may hope to know our relations and friends there.

These clear intimations of Scripture, fully meet the demands of the universal desire and expectations of mankind in regard to meeting their departed friends. It has been the general hope and belief, among men, that they will know and love their friends in the future world. "Go where we will, we find the sentiment, that friendship is perpetuated beyond the grave. It is enshrined in the heart of our common humanity. The pure, unsophisticated belief of the vast majority of the followers of Christ, is in union with the yearnings of natural affection, which follows its object through the portals of the grave into the eternal world. What but this causes the Christian parent, in the dying hour, to charge his beloved children to prepare for a reunion before the throne of the Lamb? He desires to meet them there, and to rejoice with them in the victory over sin and death. The widow, bending in bitter bereavement over the grave of him whom God has taken, meekly puts the cup of sorrow to her lips, with the assured confidence that the separation wrought by death is transient, and that they who sleep in Jesus, shall together inherit the rest that remaineth for the people of God. Thus the wormwood and the gall are tempered by the sweet balm of hope, and heaven wins the attractions which earth has lost. Tell me, ye who have seen the open tomb receive into its bosom the sacred trust committed to its keeping, in hope of the *first resurrection*,—you who have heard the sullen rumbling of the death-clods, as they dropped upon the coffin-lid, and told you that earth had gone back to earth,—when the separation from the object of your love was realized in all the desolation of bereavement, next to the thought that ere long you should see Christ as he is, and be like him, was not that consolation the strongest which assured you that the departed one, whom God has put from you into darkness, will run to meet you, when you cross the threshold of immortality, and, with the holy rapture to which the redeemed alone can give utterance, lead you to the exalted Saviour, and with you bow at his feet, and cast the conqueror's crown before him?"—*Rev. J. F. Berg.*

Dr. Chalmers says, "Tell us if Christianity does

not throw a pleasing radiance around an infant's tomb? And should any parent who hears me, feel softened by the remembrance of the light that twinkled a few short months under his roof, and at the end of its little period expired, we cannot think we venture too far when we say, that he is only to persevere in the faith, and in the following of the Gospel, and that very light will again shine upon him in heaven. The blossom which withered here upon its stalk, has been transplanted there to a place of endurance; and it will there gladden that eye which now weeps out the agony of an affection which has been sorely wounded; and, in the name of Him who, if on earth, would have wept along with them, as we bid all believers present to sorrow, not even as others which have no hope, but to take comfort in the hope of that country where there is no sorrow, and no separation." Scripture and reason, and all the aspirations of natural affection, unitedly lead us to believe that there will be a personal recognition in heaven, and an acquaintance formed with all the holy. It is true that great changes will pass upon us in our transit from mortal to immortal, and in the rapid unfolding of our powers in heaven; but these may not be more marked than the changes from infancy to manhood, and yet we recognize our friends notwithstanding all these. Our children may be so altered, that it may be necessary for some angel who has watched over them to point them out to us, and introduce them, just as is sometimes the case on earth when long separations have taken place. In forming an acquaintance, too, with Abraham, and Paul, and the innumerable company of angels and saints, it may be by regular introduction. As John the Baptist pointed out the Land of God to men, and as Gabriel announced his own name and office, to those to whom he ministered, so as we meet them they may announce themselves, or we may seek an introduction through others. To be able to recognize all, may require a long time. In fact, we may be forming new acquaintances through eternity. From different worlds there may be coming up thither new personages, with whom we may become associated in endeared intercourse. Supposing this to be true, it would give variety and freshness to our social intercourse and enjoyment.

To some the idea of personal recognition, and a renewal of acquaintance with those with whom we have been associated on earth, is by no means pleasant, and hence is rejected. Their relations in life have not been happy. Between husbands and wives, neighbors and friends, and often between the members of the same church, there has existed, in many cases, the most confirmed alienation. To such it would be more pleasing, could they be assured that they would never see or know those for whom they have had no affection, and between whom such differences have existed. But let it be remembered that none can gain admission to heaven, who have any alienation, ill-will or hatred in their hearts. If we and those with whom our relations have been unpleasant on earth, meet in heaven, we shall have left behind us all that is unlovely and unholy, and perhaps on our recognition there, our wonder, love, and joy may be the greater, when we recount together the past, and find that we have been washed and saved notwithstanding our differences. But perhaps many who hope for heaven will never get there on account of those unlovely traits which have produced alienations and contentions on earth. If we expect to meet and love in the world to come, how earnestly should we now seek to love and to cultivate all those graces which endear and strengthen affection.

But could we suppose that there would be no personal recognition in heaven, and that we should thereby avoid the renewal of those unhappy associations which have tormented us in the present world, our situation might be more wretched than it could otherwise be. For as memory would remain, we might be tantalized with the suspicion that those with whom we were associated on earth might be near us, or the very ones with whom we were conversing. It might be to us an exceedingly painful source of doubt not to know where our friends were, or by whom we were surrounded. It will, no doubt, be found upon reflection, that the simple teachings of Scripture on this subject are attended with less difficulty, and are infinitely more joyous than any other view. We could form no consistent and intelligent view of another life, as a continuation of the present, were we not permitted to believe in a full remembrance of all the past, and a perfect recognition of ourselves and others.

PARTICULAR FRIENDSHIPS IN HEAVEN.

The idea of a personal recognition in heaven, and of a reunion of those who have fondly loved on earth, often suggests the inquiry,—Will there be peculiar friendships in the future, as in the present world? or shall we be equally attached to, and interested in, all the myriads of the holy? On this point there is nothing definitely revealed in Scripture, and yet there is nothing to forbid the indulgence of a sentiment so pleasant.

The example of our Lord certainly gives some support to this view, and conclusively shows that a particular friendship is not inconsistent with the most exalted purity, and the most refined sensibility, and enlarged benevolence, in respect to all. There was one disciple whom Jesus loved—loved in a very peculiar sense, in distinction from the others. There is much prominence given to this in Scripture. It is mentioned in some six different passages. "On perusing the Evangelists, it appears that he was invariably selected by our Lord, as one of the three who were present in the most retired scenes of his life, on the Mount of Transfiguration, in the house of Jairus, and in the garden of Gethsemane. Whoever else were absent, John was sure to share his most confidential moments, and to witness his most secret joys and conflicts. At the paschal supper, to which he looked forward with so much eagerness, as the appointed season for a more unreserved disclosure of his purposes than he had made before, he placed John next to himself, in such a manner that his head naturally rested on his bosom. Through him it was that the rest of the disciples applied to our Lord, to be informed who it was that should betray him. But the most decisive evidence of the preference bestowed upon John, arises from his being chosen to take care of his widowed mother after his decease."—*R. Hall.* And so, after his resurrection and ascension, he continued to receive from his Saviour similar proofs of his preference.

Now, as Christ knew no sin, neither was guile found in his mouth, his peculiar love for John shows that a particular friendship is not inconsistent with even Divine purity, and that universal love which will flow unobstructed, and uncorrupted, from heart to heart, amid the brotherhood of heaven. We see not, then, why we may not innocently entertain the idea, that there may be some spirit or spirits in heaven, more congenial to us than others, and to whom we may be more intimately and tenderly allied.

This sentiment is rendered plausible, from the consideration that the purity of heaven will not, probably, obliterate those peculiarities of character, temperament, and taste, which are not sinful, and which are essential to our individuality. There will, no doubt, be as great a diversity in individual characteristics, sin excepted, and in gifts, as on earth. Hence, we are assured that some "shall shine as the brightness of the firmament," and others, "as the stars, forever and ever." Some will be kings, some priests unto God; and the redeemed will differ from one another, as do the stars that gem the heavens at night.

Now, these diversities, essential to heaven's order and harmony, may, and we should naturally suppose would, bring some into nearer relationship than others, and lay the foundation for peculiar attachments. It can hardly be supposed that we can be equally attached to, and equally familiar with, all the innumerable parts of the upper world, as we shall be with some few congenial spirits, who may occupy the same position and circle in which we may move.

Perhaps those whose friendship on earth has been the result of religious principle, and whose love has been cemented by the grace of our Lord Jesus Christ, amid scenes of like temptation and sorrow, will, through all the long years of eternity, cherish a peculiar love for each other. Why should they not? Is there anything in Scripture or reason to forbid it?

But let it be borne in mind, that those merely natural relationships which have existed in life, and those affections which have not been connected with, and sanctified by religion, will not be maintained hereafter. In the resurrection we shall neither marry, nor be given in marriage; but in respect to these natural relations, we shall be all as the angels of God, and equal one to another—*Luke*, 20: 36.

"It must be remembered, that, in the other world, we shall love one another, not so much on account of the relation and friendship that formerly existed between us, as on account of the knowledge and virtue that we possess; for, among rational beings, whose affections will be all suited to the high state of moral and intellectual perfection to which they shall be raised, the most endearing relations and warmest friendships will be those which are founded on excellence of character. What a powerful consideration this, to excite us to cultivate in our relations and friends the noble and lasting qualities of knowledge and virtue, which will prove such a source of happiness to them and to us, through the endless ages of eternity."—*Macknight.*

The peculiar love of our Saviour for John, was perhaps because the natural disposition of Jesus was more nearly like the amiableness and mildness of John, than any of the other disciples. Peculiar traits of character were, no doubt, the cause of it. The fictitious distinctions between the rich and the poor, the high-born and the low, will not exist hereafter. Character and likeness to Jesus will be the test, and these will constitute essential elements in all the friendships that will be formed or exist in the world to come. Hence, as all in heaven will be in the likeness of the Saviour, any peculiar friendship which may exist will not interfere with a universal love for all, any more than Christ's love for John lessened his love for the other disciples.

There is nothing revealed in Scripture which shows that heaven has any restraint from these socialities; but the example of our Saviour shadows forth the reverse. The redeemed, each "with his choice friend, his mother, brother, sister, wife, child, or with all together, may wander forth over the flowery hills and plains of glory, drawing delight from every object, discoursing of things past and present, and weighing their former sorrows against their new happiness. There the lover and his loved shall meet, who, separated by death, ere reaching the consummation of their wishes, went down to their graves with this single hope shining like a star upon them. There the Davids and the Jonathans of all ages, as faithful to God as to each other, may rise up to find their loves immortal."

There the faithful minister may meet his faithful and affectionate people, and renew those friendships which were rudely sundered in life. All the relations between man and man, which the Creator has ordained and revelation has sanctified, will there be recognized forever. All the joys of earth, social as well as personal, will be treasured there, because we cannot go to heaven without carrying our natures and our recollections with us.

This view is in harmony with all the endeared and consecrated affections and prompting of our natures, and is deeply and fondly cherished in human hearts, if not embodied in outward sentiment. Nor is it without its practical influence; for as, according to Scripture, only sanctified affections and friendships can exist in heaven—only those which bear the impress of the Holy, and are enstamped with the love of God and the Lamb—a motive, high and strong as joys above, is presented, to lead us to consecrate all to God, and to seek, by all the means and agencies within our reach, that union to heaven, and that purity of heart which will secure the blessing. "But I would not have you to be ignorant, brethren, concerning them which are asleep, that ye sorrow not, even as others which have no hope. For if we believe that Jesus died and rose again, even so them also which sleep in Jesus will God bring with him."—1 *Thess.* 4: 13, 14.

But whatever doubt may exist in the minds of any in regard to the point last discussed, it will not be disputed that there will be in heaven the

PLEASURES OF SEEING.

We shall have eyes in the world to come, and these must have objects of beauty and instruction, and grandeur upon which to look in endless variety.

It has been questioned, by some, whether we shall really see God in heaven? The Saviour said, "Blessed are the pure in heart, *for they shall see God.*" Is not this conclusive that we shall? We shall certainly see Jesus Christ, God manifest in our nature. "For we know that when he doth appear, we shall be like him; for we shall see him as he is." Our Lord also prayed, "Father I will, that these whom thou hast given me, be with me, that *they may behold my glory*."

Here the thought is distinctly brought out. A part of heaven's happiness will consist in seeing—in beholding the glory of Christ. Something more is meant in this, than that we shall see his glorified person, and the resplendent honors and beauties by which he is surrounded in heaven.

The glory of Christ is the glory of his character and infinite perfections. The glory of omnipotence, of omniscience, of omnipresence, of wisdom, and love, is his. And these in the world to come, as in this, will be displayed in the works of his hands, and those wonders he will perform through his boundless universe. "The heavens declare the glory of God and the firmament showeth his handiwork;" but all this is a part of the glory of Christ, for he made them, and for himself they were created. To behold the glory of Christ, then, will be to behold his works—the manifestation of his boundless perfections and attributes, as they will be displayed in the mansions he has gone to prepare, and through the universe of created beings which he has formed for the exhibition of himself.

We understand the passage, therefore, as clearly intimating that the boundless universe will be open to our vision, and for our investigation, from the smallest microscopic objects up to the most distant and most glorious orb which rolls in undiscovered space; for all these are the glory of Christ, and we must see them, if we behold his glory in its wide extent. It may take an eternity to see all, but we shall need to have new objects and scenes continually passing before us forever, in order to give employment to our expanding minds, and to minister to our pleasure. And God can easily give to our resurrection bodies, which will be adapted to our spiritual natures, powers of locomotion and vision which will enable us to realize all that is promised.

In these remarks we take it for granted that this glorious material universe, in the midst of which we dwell, will stand forever—that, whatever physical or geological changes may take place in revolving systems and worlds, they will still continue to roll on, declaring in their evolutions and productions the glory of their Creator and Upholder. Poets may sing of the "wreck of worlds," of "nature's funeral pile," and of the quenching of the sun and stars in endless night; but we are confidently persuaded that no such catastrophies are intimated in Scripture. The language which tells of the sun being darkened, and the stars falling from heaven, is symbolical, and was intended to represent those civil, political and ecclesiastical revolutions to take place on earth, in order to prepare the way for the coming and universal dominion of our Lord Jesus Christ.

We cannot tell what may be seen in heaven

itself, aside from the throne of God and the Lamb, and the myriads of pure worshippers who surround it. But in the unnumbered worlds which revolve around, there will be an infinite variety of objects, beautiful and grand, from the smallest microscopic insect, up to the huge leviathan that swims the flood. "There will be a solid foothold to walk on; a heavenly air to feed our inspirations; light to break in beauty upon our eyelids; sounds as soft as symphonies, to warble upon our hearing; odors sweeter than the scent of roses, fruits more fragrant than the growth of earthly paradise, and a universe of tangible objects of the fairest forms and qualities, to gratify and delight us. Grass will grow, flowers will bloom, fruits will ripen, forests will wave, rivers and rivulets will roll, high hills will tower, valleys will wind and vales expand, and, beyond them all, far as the eye can reach, vast blue oceans will forever heave, and sigh, and swell, where such as we shall go to enjoy the faculties we carry with us," and to see the wonders of God.

There may be higher, more perfect, and beautiful forms of existence in other worlds than here, which, when we see them, will fill us with adoring wonder, in view of the unlimited power, skill, and resources of the Redeemer; and which will raise our souls to higher devotion than ever to him, who, though the Creator and Ruler of all, stooped to raise us from sin, to behold and participate in his glory. The Saviour, when on earth, pointed to bird and flower, to things animate and inanimate, to illustrate the wisdom, power, and goodness of God. Why may he not in other worlds, and amid higher scenes? All this may present no attractions to those who have now no taste for the beauties of nature, or disposition to receive pleasure from the study and contemplation of the works of God. But if any do not now see and enjoy God in his works, it is owing to some defect in early training, or some unfortunate bias of mind, which will most certainly be corrected, in all who truly love the Creator, and delight in his purity. In the society and amid the communings of heaven, there will undoubtedly be

PLEASURES OF HEARING.

Much of the pleasure and enjoyment of life results from hearing. It will be so in the world to come. This is not conjecture. It is so written. How often, in the Revelations, do we hear the disciple saying, "And I heard a great voice." "And I heard the voice of many angels round about the throne." "And I heard the voice of harpers, harping with their harps: and they sang as it were a new song before the throne." There will be music to be heard. This has been truly styled the "divine art." Disconnected from the impure thoughts and words of men, it is as immaculate as heaven's own light. It has powers to enchant and elevate the soul almost to heavenly rapture, even amid the imperfections and discords of earth. This divine art will not be lost or be silent in heaven. There will be instruments and songs there, such as earth has never heard.

In the resurrection state, when these vile bodies shall be fashioned like unto Christ's glorious body, and these harps, of a thousand strings, shall be retuned to heaven's harmonies, there will be music performed through material organs as now, and giving utterance to the devotions and joys of sinless souls, which will ravish the ear and heart with joys unspeakable. But it is a vain and irrational conceit of some, to suppose that we shall be continually singing through eternity. Our songs of praise there will be intelligent, and will, probably, be called forth, from time to time, by new manifestations and discoveries of the perfections of God, which we shall learn in beholding the glory of Christ. To those who have no ear or taste for music now, the idea that there will be singing in heaven, conveys no emotion of pleasure. But let such remember that our senses will then all be perfect, and those who cannot now sing, through a defective ear, will as easily as others catch the notes of the redeemed. How pleasant it will be for those who have worshipped together on earth, to meet occasionally in some social gathering in another life, and in recounting the past, to unite in singing *Old* Hundred, or some other equally famed melody of earth! It may be so—we believe it will.

But music will not be all that will be heard. In our social intercourse we shall hear the speech of angels, the communings of patriarchs and prophets, and the voice of friendship and love. Lessons of deepest wisdom we may learn, from hearing archangels and others relate their experience, or rehearse the wonders they have seen of the manifestations of God, in distant worlds and times. And above all, we shall hear the instructions of the Lamb, who will feed us and lead us to fountains of living water, and whose kindness and love will wipe away every tear from every eye.—*Rev.* 7 : 17. From the clear revelations of Scripture, we may certainly look for, in the world to come, the

PLEASURES OF INCREASING KNOWLEDGE.

It is admitted that the mind of man is susceptible of indefinite improvement, and of constantly increasing knowledge. This clearly intimates its future destiny, and points out its eternal and glorious career. It would be a sad and gloomy prospect for the future, were we to remain, through an endless life, as ignorant as we now are, and as narrowly contracted in our views.

To be truly happy, we shall need to be forever progressing in knowledge and improvement. Now, that which is here suggested as essential to our future blessedness, by the demands and capacities of the mind, is fully confirmed by the assurances of the lively oracles.

Our Lord said to his disciples, *John*, 13 : 7, "What

I do thou knowest not now; but thou shalt know hereafter." That is, the reasons and the grand results of that which I now do, thou knowest not; but you shall know it all *hereafter*, in another life.

1 *Cor.* 13: 12, "For now we see through a glass, darkly; but then face to face: now I know in part; but then shall I know even as also I am known."

1 *Cor.* 4: 5, "Therefore judge nothing before the time, *until the Lord come,* who both will bring to light the hidden things of darkness, and will make manifest the counsels of the hearts."

These Scriptures clearly assert a vastly increased knowledge in a future state, even a perfect and satisfactory knowledge of those dark and mysterious things which are now connected in our feeble understandings, with the character, and government, and works of God. The mysteries of God will then be finished, *Rev.* 10: 7, and through that long day of eternity there will be such unfoldings of the infinite mind externally, in his revelations and works, as will fill all with admiration, joy, and praise.

"We have now a sure work of prophecy; whereunto ye do well that ye take heed, as unto a light that shineth in a dark place, until the day dawn, and the day star arise in your hearts." 2 *Pet.* 1: 19.

How beautifully and grandly expressive this passage. The light which we now enjoy in the written word, compared with that light or knowledge we shall enjoy when the bright sun of an eternal day shall burst in cloudless glory upon us, is only like the dim lamp or candle that shines in a dark room, compared with the glories of a full orbed day, which sheds its effulgence over a universe.

We are justified then, from the Scriptures, in reckoning upon the pleasures of increasing knowledge through the boundless future. The development of the mind in endless succession will require this increase, and the heaven of heavens, and the boundless universe illuminated with the glory of God, will supply an ample field where this knowledge may be gathered, and whence this pleasure may be derived. And as it seems to be a law of heaven, that God is to be known through the works of his hands, and through the judgments he has wrought, it is a just inference, that in eternity, as here, our knowledge will be acquired by the exercise of our rational faculties, in connection with his works. Every power of the mind will then be called into action, and will find delightful employment in those fields and pursuits in which love divine may direct. And we have no reason to suppose that our progress will be so slow and wearisome as now. The contrary is affirmed. "Not only the qualities, but the essence of all things may then be plain. The close connections, the nice dependencies, the several links in the august chain of beings, as well as of causes and events, will stand out revealed. Questions discussed here for ages, and without success, will there be settled at a glance. Memory, reason, imagination, every intellectual faculty, will there be fully occupied; the work of expanding these several powers, with every other susceptibility of our nature, will be prominent in our employment; and this self-education, by those means of which heaven will be full, will every hour bring us to behold, in creation's thousand objects, more and more of God, and to know more and more of him who will be ever incomprehensible.

But as the exercise of our powers and the acquisition of knowledge will not be selfish, we may anticipate in the world to come the

PLEASURES OF DOING GOOD.

We have reason to believe that much of heaven's happiness will consist in performing kind offices for others good, and in receiving theirs in return.

Be not shocked, kind reader, at this announcement. You have perhaps contemplated heaven only as a place of inactive rest, where, wandering in flowery fields, you might bask, as the sensual reptile in the sunshine, and drink of the bliss which might be furnished you from angelic cups, without any effort or exercise of your own. Or, may be, you have only thought of sitting down on cushioned seats, or standing up amid a great crowd to gaze in awe and wonder on some visible halo of glory around the throne, and singing psalms through eternity. But is any such view of heaven Scriptural or rational? Let us look at some of its clear intimations and revelations.

1. In the Scriptures, all heaven, from the great

Creator, downward through all subordinate beings, is represented as actively engaged in doing good. "My Father," said the Saviour, "worketh hitherto and I work." From the creation of the world God has been actively engaged in doing good to his creatures, in all the laws of his government, and in all the operations of his providence; and it will be necessary for him still to work through all the long ages of eternity, to satisfy the wants of every living thing. "The Creator of the ends of the earth fainteth not, neither is weary!"

The Saviour, too, has ever been actively employed. On earth he went about doing good. In heaven he now lives to make intercession, and has gone to prepare mansions for those who love him. And then through all the long future the people of God shall hunger and thirst, and want and suffer no more, "For the Lamb which is in the midst of the throne shall feed them, and shall lead them unto living fountains of waters: and God shall wipe away all tears from their eyes." *Rev.* 7 : 17.

And then the angels, too, what are they doing? Are they not all ministering spirits, sent fort to minister for them who shall be heirs of salvation?" *Heb.* 1 : 14. And will they ever cease or wish to cease the blest employment?

Now, we have a right to infer from all this, that there must, and will be, some good for the saved to do in the world to come. If not, they will be in this respect wholly unlike God, unlike the Saviour, unlike the angels. But we are told definitely, that we are to be like Christ, and in the resurrection to be equal unto the angels; and shall we not share in their blessedness of doing good? Where among all the works or creatures of God is to be found that which is always receiving, but nothing returning, except among the lost? The saints would constitute an anomaly in God's universe, were it true that in heaven they would be the constant recipients of blessings, and yet not be blessings to others in return.

2. We infer that there will be some great deeds of kindness and goodness to be done, by the saints in the various departments of the universal kingdom of their Lord, *from the high* and responsible offices they are to fill and sustain.

Rev. 1 : 6, "Unto him that loved us and washed us from our sins in his own blood, and hath made us *kings* and *priests* unto God." *Rev.* 5 : 9, 10, "And they sung a new song, saying, thou art worthy to take the book, and to open the seals thereof: for thou wast slain, and hast redeemed us unto God by thy blood out of every kindred, and tongue, and people, and nation; and *hast made us unto God kings and priests: and we shall reign on the earth.*"

"To him that overcometh will I grant to sit with me on my throne, even as I also overcame, and am set down with my father in his throne." *Rev.* 3 : 21.

Here, then, are high offices designated to be sustained by the redeemed, in the kingdom of the Redeemer. In some sense they are to be sharers with him in the honors of his throne, and in the execution of that government which is to extend its happy influence over all the good. If we are to be kings, then there must be something, or somebody over whom we shall reign; and if we are to be priests, then there must be somebody to whom we are to minister for their good—as the angels now minister to us.

There would be no force in these official designations, were there no good or service for us to perform in the future world. These Scriptures represent heaven to us as a world of subordinations, and dependencies, in which all will be employed in higher or lower stations in laboring for, and ministering to each other's good.

Kings will then reign, not for personal grandeur, but for the good of others in some department of the universe; and priests will minister, only to be the instruments of communicating to those to whom they may be sent. "He that is greatest among you let him be your servant."

3. In harmony with these unmistakable Scriptural intimations, we infer that one part of heaven's employment and enjoyment will consist in doing good, from the fact that the universal love which we are now required to cultivate for all, in preparation for the world to come, and the good works we are continually called upon to perform in view of the same great end, are adapted to prepare us for these services.

It will not be disputed that we are most clearly and earnestly required in Scripture to do good unto all men, to feed the hungry, to clothe the naked, to visit the sick, the widow and the fatherless in their affliction, and even to bless them that curse us, to do good to them that hate us, and to pray for them that despitefully use and persecute us, *that we* may be the children of our Father in heaven, and thus be fitted for his service hereafter.

We know there can be no religion in this world, and no *true* enjoyment of religion, except in the exercise of benevolent affections going out in benevolent effort for others good. The religion which does not lead to this is false and delusive. Now, why does God impart to us a religion which leads us to love and do good to others, and why does he require us to do this continually in view of the rewards of eternity, if there is no good to be performed in another life? Throughout the kingdom of God there is a wise adaptation of means to an end. Nothing is made or done in vain. And if this same law is to prevail in the future, we may safely infer, that the love which our Lord requires us now to possess, and the benevolent effort he now unceasingly calls upon us to make, clearly intimate a service of a similar character to be performed in the world to come, for which the present is preparatory.

The powers possessed, and exercised, and developed in childhood and youth, are only preparatory to their exercise in after-life. So must all that we now possess, be called into action, in future.

4. The same conclusion is drawn from the fact that *to the truly good and benevolent*, there is no hap-

piness in the present world, equal to that derived from doing good. Our Lord Jesus said, "It is more blessed to give than to receive." Was this intended for earth only, or was it designed to teach us that everywhere, and in any world, there is more blessedness to be received from giving or doing good, than from receiving? And shall God shut us out from the greater good in the world to come, and make us there only the receivers, and not the promoters of good? Shall this be the employment of God—the Redeemer, through eternity, and of his angels, and yet his saints have no participation in this his highest joy? Shall his people be workers together with him here on earth, and yet be excluded in the higher life? O where then will be the outgoings of our love? And how will those benevolent graces and characters which we are now required so earnestly to seek, find appropriate development and exercise? Now, to us it seems clear from the fact, that the more pure and benevolent and godlike we become on earth, the more we long and desire to do good, and the more pleasure we take in acts of true beneficence, that such, in a high degree, will be the nature of our employments in heaven; and from this, one source of our highest enjoyment will be derived. Viewed in this light,—

"This world's not all a fleeting show,
For man's illusion given;
He that hath sooth'd a widow's woe,
Or wip'd an orphan's tear, doth know
There's something *here* of Heaven.

"And he that walks life's thorny way,
With feelings calm and even,
Whose path is lit from day to day,
By virtue's bright and steady ray,
Hath something *felt* of Heaven.

"He that the Christian's course hath run,
And all his foes forgiven,
Who measures out life's little span
In love to God, and love to man,
On *earth* hath tasted Heaven."

We need not, then, really wait for heaven in another life. In proportion as we become like God, and engage in the great work in which he is ever employed, heaven will come down to greet and cheer us here. All nature then, in harmony with the promptings of eternal love, seems clearly to point out man's future and beneficent career.

"The rolling waves, the sun's unwearied course,
The elements and seasons, all declare
For what the Eternal Maker has ordained
The powers of man: we feel within ourselves
His energy divine: He tells the heart
He meant, He made us to behold and love
What he beholds and loves, the general orb
Of life and being: to be great like him,
Beneficent and active."

Should any ask what good there will be to be done in the world to come, among the saved, where all will be holy and happy, we answer, The fact that we cannot tell, furnishes no argument against the view presented. We could easily conjecture enough that might and could be done in entire harmony with the perfection and blessedness of heaven, and yet as it is not written out, it might, or it might not be, just as we supposed. According to the millenarian view of the world to come, the saints, under Christ, are to judge or rule over the world, and are to be his ministers, to execute his loving kindness to the ceaseless generations who shall be born, and ripen for higher spheres. According to this view, we shall be employed hereafter in the same blessed work, only in a higher and more blessed state, that our trials and characters fit us for here on earth.

But suppose this view of the subject is not correct, and that in the immediate vicinity of the throne, and in the midst of the great congregation in which we shall assemble from time to time, there will be no special good for us to do to others, still in this wide universe, and amid these worlds that roll around us, there may be room enough for the exercise of all our powers, and objects enough upon which our tenderest sympathies and warmest affections may be lavished in doing good. God may send us, as he now sends the angels to our world, to other and far-off worlds, to guide and teach and train those inferior to ourselves for the higher allotments of their being. We need not fear that God cannot find full employment for all the faculties he has given us, and for all the pure affections and graces he has trained us to amid life's trials. O what a motive to cultivate benevolent affections and the love of doing good is here presented. The view taken is full of practical and benign importance. Out then ye idle and selfish, and be doing, or heaven may never be yours.

From this view of the employments of the redeemed, we may turn and contemplate the joyous

CONVOCATIONS OF HEAVEN.

It is clearly revealed that the worship of God and the Lamb in heaven will constitute a prominent source of enjoyment. This will not be doubted. Some speak and write of heaven, as if every moment there would be unceasingly employed in acts of adoration and praise to the great Eternal. But such are not the intimations of Scripture, or the suggestions of reason. Heaven, we doubt not, will have her Sabbaths—her seasons of great and holy convocation, regularly returning, when the great congregation shall assemble from the various departments of the better land, and from all the outposts and stations of the kingdom, in the great temple of Jehovah, reared by his own hand, and garnished with his own fingers, to engage in social and united thanksgiving and praise.

In the first and second chapters of the Book of Job, we read that, "*there was a day*," a set time, "*when the sons of God come to present themselves before the Lord.*" It is generally understood that by the sons of God here are meant the angels. It seems, then, that the angels have a day or set time in which to present themselves before the Lord. And if such a season, regularly returning, is appointed for the angels, why may we not conclude that there will be for the redeemed, who in the resurrection are to be made like unto the angels? That, as in Zion of old, emblem of the holy, there will be great festive occasions, when the tribes of the Lord will go up to worship, to recount their joys and the wondrous displays of love, wisdom, and power, they have witnessed in those departments where it has been their honor and happiness to minister? Such an idea is more pleasant and rational than any other. We doubt not that heaven will have her Sabbaths—when, during eternal ages, every occupation will cease, "while angel and archangel, and patriarch, and prophet, and apostle, and every order, class, grade, and tribe of heaven's busy multitudes will come from every region, thronging to the mount of worship, where the throne is set—where the martyrs stand—where the elders sit—where the harpers harp—where the company of the singers shout—where the lightnings and thunders are mingled with the sound of the trumpet —where the voice of every creature that is in heaven, and on the earth, and under the earth, and such as are in the sea, and of all that are in them, are heard, saying, "Blessing, and honor, and glory, and power, be unto Him that sitteth upon the throne, and unto the Lamb forever and ever." And here, as mind kindles mind, and heart warms to heart, and eye sparkles with exulting joy to eye, will burst forth those rapturous songs, led on, may be, by sainted bards of old, which will fill all heaven with unutterable delights, and inspire the worshippers to higher and more ardent zeal in the service of their Lord.

This view is not contradicted by the passage in *Rev.* 4 : 8, which represents the four living creatures, having each six wings, and full of eyes within, as resting not day and night, saying, "Holy, holy, holy, Lord God Almighty." These creatures are symbolical, and of course their acts are symbolical also, and they were never intended to represent literally the employments of the redeemed through unending ages. And yet viewing them as the symbols or representatives of the redeemed, their acts may represent the spirit which will pervade their minds at every step of their progress. Amid the hosts of heaven, everything will be done in the service of God. Whether ruling as kings, or ministering as priests, all will be in love and obedience to Jehovah; and at every step and turn they will see his glory, and in spirit, say "Holy, holy, holy, Lord God Almighty, the whole universe is full of his glory."

O my soul, what scenes and joys are in reserve! And shall earth allure thee, and unfit thee for devotions and services so pure and lovely?

DIFFERENT DEGREES OF GLORY IN HEAVEN.

The opinion has been entertained by some, that as all are saved by grace, all in heaven will be equally rewarded; and, hence, that there will be no different degrees in glory. But this is unscriptural. The angel revealed to *Daniel*, 12 : 3, that "they that be wise, shall shine as the brightness of the firmament; *and they that turn many to righteousness, as the stars forever and ever.*" This passage shows that those who are most eminently useful will occupy a higher position in heaven, than those who are simply pious.

In the parable of the talents, *Luke*, 19 : 12-27, our Lord teaches, that there will be very different degrees in the rewards bestowed. To some will be given authority over ten cities, to others five, and to others two, according to their fidelity in improving that committed to them.

In other Scriptures we are taught that some are to be kings, and some priests unto God—showing a wide difference in the official stations, which the redeemed will fill.

It is also affirmed, as a universal principle of rectitude in the judgments of the world to come, that all, the righteous as well as the wicked, will be rewarded according to their works. Now, it follows from this, that as some good people make far greater attainments in holiness in this world than others, and do vastly more to bless mankind, and honor God, their reward must be proportionally greater. It is true they, as well as others, are accepted in the beloved; but in Christ, God has been pleased to hold out this incentive of an increased glorious reward to the faithful, to stimulate and encourage them to every good word and work.

And, then, can any reasonably suppose that he who has just religion enough to get into heaven, will have as bright a crown, and occupy as exalted a position as Paul, who devoted long years of affectionate labor, amid trials and sufferings, to the cause of the Redeemer. Will those who have lived at home, and at their ease, and made no self-denying sacrifices for others' good, be on an equality with those devoted missionaries who, amid great trials and sufferings, have gone into the dark places of the earth to preach the unsearchable riches of Christ? Will the idler in God's spiritual vineyard, receive the same as the devoted and zealous? To suppose such a thing, would be most unreasonable and unjust, as well as unscriptural.

But according to a very obvious law of human minds, there will be a necessity for different degrees in heaven. It is quite certain that the more an individual's mind is expanded by love, virtue, and knowledge in the present world, the higher, in the world to come, will be the point from which he will commence his upward and onward progress during eternal ages. He will be prepared, in the beginning, for a higher position, and for greater enjoyments than others, who have had less love, less holiness, and less divinely-inspired knowledge than he. There will, no doubt, be many very striking reverses even in heaven. The slave may there be above his master, and the servant above his lord. Not in all cases those who have been most distinguished and honored on earth, will be most renowned hereafter. The poor, in many instances, will there have the pre-eminence. God will exalt the lowly. Those who have been most humble, most pure, most self-denying for others' good, and who have contended most earnestly, even unto death, striving against sin, will receive a crown of life most resplendent. Knowledge unsanctified, and perverted to selfish, base, and ambitious ends, will not avail in the future. It must be connected with justice, mercy, and the love of God and man, or it will only be as a mill-stone about our neck, to sink us in deep waters of sorrow. It is to be feared that many will be vast losers to all eternity, from inattention to the clearly-revealed truth under consideration, and indolence, negligence, and unbelief in the great work of life given us to do. It is only by giving diligence to add to all our virtues, that an *abundant entrance* will be administered to us into the everlasting kingdom of our Lord and Saviour Jesus Christ. 2 *Peter*, 1 : 5–11.

HEAVEN INCOMPREHENSIBLE.

But after all that has been written, it may emphatically be said, "It doth not yet appear what we shall be," though there are some things definitely revealed. The things which are unseen are eternal. But what finite mind can comprehend eternity? Think of as many years as there are stars in the sky; as many ages as there are sands on the ocean shore; as many cycles of ages as there are spires of grass on earth's wide surface; and then run over all these again, as many times as there are leaves in all the forests of the world, and had you a mind capable of summing up the vast amount, there would still be an eternity unlimited, stretching in the expanding future. The child of a few years old, could not understand his short earthly existence, were it minutely told him. His faculties and experience would not be large enough to grasp his three score years and ten. How then can we, a few years older, comprehend what we shall be or enjoy through an infinite duration? We could not were it all revealed. We should not have time to read it. It would take an eternity. Hence the great outline is only given. The filling up is reserved for actual experience in the unfoldings of an endless life. Hence, any one might ask a thousand questions about the minutia of the world to come, and our progress through unending years, which cannot be answered because not revealed, and which could not be appreciated, if they were, because not now able to see all their bearings and relations. There are deep mysteries hanging about our present and future existence, which the wisest cannot penetrate. It is only our faith in God, in the benevolence of his character, and in the universal and eternal rectitude of his government, that can give us rest and peace on the rolling billows of the ocean of life, and as we look into the mysteries of the future. Faith we need now, and faith we shall need through eternity. All this does not detract from heaven. There is a pleasure in mystery, in the longings and anticipations it excites. Enough, however, is revealed to satisfy all the reasonable demand and aspirations of our natures—enough to show us that heaven has attractions infinitely transcending anything which this world can give or take away—enough to assure us that every want of our souls will there be met, that every desire will be gratified—every longing filled—every pain assuaged—all tears wiped away, and all that can hurt or destroy subdued.

And now let it come to every heart, as a personal and momentous inquiry, Is heavenly happiness mine? Am I prepared for it? Am I living in view of it, and acting in reference to it? Am I, in dependence on God, and according to his Gospel, seeking to form and cultivate a character in harmony with it? The question is soon to be settled, whether this heaven shall be ours or not. What amazing interests are at stake?

> "How much is to be done! My hopes and fears
> Start up alarm'd, and o'er life's narrow verge
> Look down—on what? A fathomless abyss;
> A dread eternity! how surely mine!
> And can eternity belong to me,
> Poor pensioner on the bounties of an hour?"

O what a loss it will be to miss such a heaven as is revealed. Reader, it is possible, it may be lost. Just as you may lose any earthly happiness, by neglecting to seek it in the appointed time and way.

How many destroy their peace, and character, and happiness in the present life, and involve themselves in inextricable ruin. It is just as possible to do it in reference to the world to come. It would be contrary to all reason and analogy were it not so. Who is willing to run the risk? There is only one right way. "The path of the just is as the shining light, which shineth more and more unto the perfect day." "Mark the perfect man, and behold the upright, for the end of that man is peace." The apostle John assures us that "Every man that hath this hope in him purifieth himself, even as he is pure." "How can two walk together except they be agreed?" We must be like Jesus, and like heaven in character, or we could not be happy were we admitted there. Reader, are you ready?

CHAPTER VII.

THE NATURE OF FUTURE PUNISHMENT.

"And chiefly thou, O Spirit, that doest prefer
Before all temples, the upright heart and pure,
Instruct me, for thou knowest:—
—— What in me is dark
Illumine; what is low, raise and support—
That to the height of this great argument
I may assert eternal Providence,
And justify the ways of God to men."—MILTON.

THE only spot in the world to come, which is not delightfully attractive, is hell. But even this may have attractions for all whom heaven owns or draws not, if not pleasant or willing. As gravitation draws bodies within its influence to earth, as the cess-pool gathers in its cavity the sediment conveyed in drains. as the grave claims, and the worm revels in the dead, and as the unsanctified usually seek their place and pleasures away from the sanctuary, and the love, and the service of God—so, naturally, and by an inevitable law of nature and sin, may hell draw the wicked to its dark domain, and bury in its grave, in which the worm never dies, the morally and spiritually dead.

Refuse, not, friend, to read, to consider, to ponder. It may do thee good. If hell has no pleasing attractions—if it is indeed a dark spot in the moral landscape of the future world—a deep and miry morass, in which those who sink rise no more—it has powers to warn, to entreat, to persuade from sin. "The prudent man forseeth the evil, and hideth himself." Why should not the sinner? If the dark storm was gathering around you, would you shut your eyes to dangers, and close your ears to the warnings of the distant warring elements, and not rather seek a shelter? Were you in the midst of the pestilence, would you remain indifferent, or would you not rather flee from before it to some secure retreat; or, if taken, provide yourself immediately with an effectual remedy?

Hell may be avoided. There is a high-way—a glorious highway around it, laid out by the Lord of glory, and paved with infinite love, and guarded by the perfections and angels of God. It is the highway of holiness. "The unclean shall not pass over it; no lion shall be there, nor any ravenous beast shall go up thereon, it shall not be found there; but the redeemed shall walk there: and the ransomed of the Lord shall return, and come to Zion with songs and everlasting joy upon their heads: they shall attain joy and gladness, and sorrow and sighing shall flee away." O wicked, turn ye into the way of life. Enter into the gate of heaven—the straight gate, which opens unto the path of obedience, purity, and unending glory. "Let the wicked forsake his way, and the unrighteous man his thoughts; and let him return unto the Lord, who will have mercy upon him; and unto our God, for he will abundantly pardon." *Is.* 55: 7.

That you may be intelligently persuaded to do this, and understand definitely what it is that you are called upon to shun, and be able to appreciate the justice and benevolence of God in the sufferings of the lost, it is proposed to discuss particularly, the nature of future punishment, as revealed in Scripture, and show its consistency with the character, government and benevolence of Jehovah.

The limits assigned to this subject will not allow us to consider particularly the Scriptural proofs of the reality of a future punishment.

Taking this point for granted, except as it may be incidentally sustained by passages adduced for other purposes, the question proposed is, *What is the nature of that punishment* which God has threatened to inflict upon the disobedient and impenitent?

THE IMPORTANCE OF THE SUBJECT.

This is not an idle question, having no beneficial or practical bearings. It is vitally important to a correct understanding of the character and government of God. A knowledge of the criminal laws of any government, and of the punishments inflicted upon transgressors, is necessary to enable us to form a correct estimate of its character, and of the justice and benevolence of its rulers. Should some government or prince, within our knowledge, inflict its punishments, as do the savages, by studying to produce the greatest amount of personal suffering; and should another, pursuing a more humane policy, simply shut criminals up by themselves where they could do no harm, and there suffer them to reap the fruit of their own doings; our judgments and feelings in respect to their character, and our acquiescence in their laws, would be very materially affected. In the light of civilization and benevolence, and according to the constitution of our minds, we could not but approve the one, and condemn the other.

So as we are called upon cheerfully to submit to the government of God, cordially to approve and acquiesce in his decisions, and willingly and joyfully to yield to his sway, it is important that we should understand, definitely, if possible, the demands of his lòve, the rewards he will bestow upon the righteous, and the nature of the punishments which will be inflicted on transgressors.

Extravagant and unscriptural views in regard to the nature of future punishment, have disgusted and driven thousands into infidelity and other errors, who might have been won to the love and obedience of the truth by more Scriptural and rational convictions.

Imagination or superstition are of no authority here. If we have no right to take from, we must be equally careful not to add to that which is revealed. It is our privilege humbly to inquire what has God taught?

To present this subject as clearly as possible, and

for the purpose of refuting some prevalent errors, it is proposed, *First*, to consider some of those things which do not constitute or enter into the nature of future punishment; and, *Secondly*, in what, according to the various representation of Scripture, it does consist.

The future punishment threatened is manifestly

NOT ANNIHILATION.

The belief that annihilation, or an entire extinction of conscious existence, is the peculiar punishment of sin threatened in Scripture, has been greatly revived of late, and is more extensively held than is supposed by those who have not had the opportunity of knowing. It will be proper, therefore, to notice it, in attempting to determine what are the teachings of the Word of God. It must be admitted that there are passages which, taken separately, very naturally suggest the idea; but then the Scriptures must be consistent with themselves, and harmonious; and hence, when an interpretation is given of certain passages which brings them into collision with others, equally clear in their statements, it is certain that such an interpretation is wrong.

1. An indiscriminate annihilation of the wicked, however diversified their characters and crimes, cannot be the punishment threatened; because the Scriptures uniformly declare that God will, in the

awards of the world to come, render to every man according to his works. It will not be necessary to quote the passages which affirm this. They are many. We cannot conceive of any principle of government more just, or equitable. But how could the guilty be rewarded according to their works, were all punished alike? It is obvious that if one man is fifty times more wicked than another, he must receive fifty times more punishment, or they could not be dealt with according to their deeds. To render to all men alike, however various their degrees of guilt, would be as palpably unjust, as to punish the less guilty more than the greatest sinners. There is a great variety of character among men, and as great a variety in the degrees of guilt attached to each one. In the judgment of God, therefore, there must be a discrimination, and awards must be rendered equally various, or the great principle of the Divine government, giving to every one according to the deeds done in the body, must be subverted. But annihilation is one and the same thing to all—therefore to annihilate all the wicked indiscriminately would be treating them all alike, and would be in plain and open contradiction to all those Scriptures which teach that punishments will be various—that some should be be beaten with many, and some with few stripes, *Luke* 12: 47, "And that it shall be more tolerable for Tyre and Sidon, and for Sodom and Gomorrah, in the day of judgment, than for Chorazin, Bethsaida, and Capernaum, *Matt.* 10: 15. And that the scribes and Pharisees were to receive the greater condemnation, *Matt.* 23 : 14. These things could not be true, were annihilation the future punishment of the wicked.

To all this it has sometimes been replied, that the wicked will be rewarded according to their works, in that they will suffer various degrees of torment in the fires or miseries which will attend the process of annihilation. But this is to make the threatened punishment to consist, not in annihilation, but in the suffering preceding it. Were this true, the fact would be sufficient to show that future punishment will not be annihilation. If these prior sufferings were intense, and were aggravated in proportion to the guilt of men, then annihilation would be no punishment, but would come in as a kind deliverer —a sweet and longed-for release.

2. It is clear that annihilation cannot be the future punishment threatened in Scripture, because it contradicts all those passages which represent future punishment as consisting in some kind of actual misery. It is not the design to speak of the nature of this misery in this connection. This will be considered in another place. The fact that there will be some kind of positive suffering is all that is insisted on. In proof, such passages as these might be referred to, "And the smoke of their torment ascendeth up forever and ever." "And there shall be weeping and wailing and gnashing of teeth." "Where their worm dieth not, and the fire is not quenched." But there can really be no misery or torment in an-

nihilation. The momentary dread which the wicked may feel, according to this theory, and which *is not annihilation*, will be no more than the dread of a beast an instant before death. But when the deed is done, and we sink into nothing, it will be as though we never were. We shall lie quiet and peaceful, while the wave of oblivion rolls eternally over us. No one is conscious of anything before he was born. Nor will he be after he ceases to exist. What punishment or misery can there be to any when they are not? You might as well talk of punishing empty space, or imaginary phantoms, as to talk of inflicting misery on men by annihilation. Hence it may be clearly seen that this idea is wholly incompatible with the representations of Scripture respecting future misery, and it therefore cannot be true. The Word must be consistent with itself; and as shown above, when any interpretation brings one part into collision with another, it must be erroneous.

3. *The death threatened in Scripture as the peculiar penalty of sin*, does not teach or imply annihilation. "The wages of sin is death."—*Rom.* 6 : 23. "The soul that sinneth, it shall die."

Now, there is not a fact in nature that shows that death does, or can annihilate anything. Death is simply a dissolution or separation. In regard to the body, when its work is completed, it only dissolves it into its separate elements. It separates the parts of which it is composed. It does not annihilate a single particle. All remain. Does it then extinguish the rational and thinking principle? Certainly there is nothing in the import of death, or in the results which follow, which indicate such an annihilation. The most natural and obviously Scriptural idea of death, is a separation—it separates soul and body. "Then shall the dust return unto the earth as it was: and the spirit shall return unto God who gave it." *Ecc.* 12 : 7.

It is because death is a separation that the wages or punishment of sin is termed death. Sin will separate the sinner from the presence of God—from heaven, its society, and blest and holy enjoyments. This separation will be the wages—the natural and legitimate effect of sin. It is therefore *death*, in its very appropriate sense. Between death then, and annihilation, there is not a shadow of resemblance. The one properly considered does not suggest the other. It would be extremely hazardous to build a hope of an escape from future misery on an inference so illogical.

4. *The words destroy, destruction, and others of like import*, so repeatedly used in Scripture, in describing future punishment, do not teach or imply annihilation. "To destroy," as understood in all languages, "is only to change the mode or condition of existence in such a manner as to disqualify, disable, or prevent that which is destroyed, from answering the condition or end for which it was designed. When, for example, a city is said to be destroyed by a siege or an earthquake, the meaning is not that the

substances of which it is built are annihilated, but that they are so changed in condition and relationship, that they are no longer applicable to the uses for which they were erected. There may be vast remains of walls, temples, fortresses, palaces, theatres, and other structures that may continue to stand for ages almost without dilapidation. Yet the city is said to be destroyed, because it is so marred and demolished as to prevent its being used for the purposes for which it was designed—and such is its meaning generally."

So, also, we say that men are destroyed, when they are disqualified or disabled from answering the high end of their being. When applied to future punishment it has the same general and significant import. God made men to be happy, but sin renders them miserable, and thus defeats the end for which they were designed, and destroys them. God made men to answer high and holy purposes in heaven; but on account of the moral ruin which wickedness accomplishes in them, they are unfitted to answer the purposes for which they were made, and they are therefore truthfully said to be destroyed. It is said that the wicked will be destroyed hereafter, because, on account of their sinful characters, and the condition in which they will be placed, they will be disabled and cut off from the end at which they aimed, —which is happiness in sin and alienation from God. The nature of this ruin will be discussed more fully in another place, and therefore we shall not enlarge. There is nothing in language, in Scripture or reason, which shows that to be destroyed is to be annihilated.

The passage in the fourth chapter of Malachi is often referred to, to prove the utter annihilation of the wicked. "For behold, the day cometh, that shall burn as an oven; and all the proud, yea, all that do wickedly, shall be stubble: and the day that cometh shall burn them up, saith the Lord of hosts, that it shall leave them neither root nor branch."

But we deny that this passage has any reference to future punishment, any more than to any judgment or destruction by which men are removed from earth. The inhabitants of Sodom and Gomorrah were burned up root and branch, and yet they were not annihilated. The flood swept away the old world, but not one intelligent existence was extinguished. So it is predicted, in the above passage, that the day or time is coming, when all wicked men, who are too depraved to be reclaimed, and who will not submit to the Lord, shall be destroyed from off the face of the earth, in order that our world may become an abode of righteous people only. This destruction is often referred to in the prophets; but when it comes it will be no more an annihilation, than is the death of any man. There will only be a separation between soul and body. The thinking principle will still survive and live on forever.

5. It is contrary to all that we know of the works and operations of God, that anything should ever be annihilated.

It is a well-established principle in science, that no particle of matter is ever annihilated. All the manifestations in the natural world show that matter, in undergoing its various transformations and changes, loses none of its substances. It may be decomposed, may enter into a variety of new combinations, may be changed from solid to liquid, and from liquid to invisible gases, and yet not an atom be annihilated.

We may take water, and resolve it into two substances, that bear no resemblance to the original, hydrogen and oxygen gases, and then burn them up, and yet nothing is lost. They may still be retained and reunited again into water. There is no such thing as annihilation known in the material universe. How do we know, then, that there is in the spiritual? All the facts within the range of our knowledge is against such an assumption.

We have in general just as good evidence of the existence of mind, as we have of matter. We know matter from its properties, and this is about all we do know. Ask the wisest man, what is matter? And he can only define it to you by its properties. He tells you matter is that which possesses certain essential or inherent properties, such as figure, divisibility, impenetrability, mobility, extension, inertia, and attraction. That is material which manifests any one or more of these properties. The existence of material bodies is, then, known only by their manifested properties. Now, we have the same evidence in kind of the existence of mind. We know mind by its essential properties. It thinks, judges, reasons; it loves and hates. Thought, then, reason and affection, variously exercised, are the properties of a living soul, and point out its existence as certainly as matter is indicated by those properties which are peculiar to it. Matter cannot think, judge, reason, or love. These are spiritual properties, and belong only to the soul.

Now, as it is a settled, demonstrated fact in science, that no particle of matter ever is annihilated, in all the changes through which it passes, or the different forms it takes, may we not conclude that the mind, which has its own distinct properties, is never annihilated? It would certainly be contrary to all that we know of the operations of God in the natural world, to suppose it ever would be. There are no facts, then, within the range of human knowledge, upon which to base an opinion, that man's spiritual nature will ever cease to exist. We judge, therefore, that the idea of an annihilation of the wicked is contrary to Scripture and reason. It would certainly be madness for any rational being to rest a hope of an escape from future misery, on a foundation so uncertain, to say the least, and neglect that cultivation of character which is essential to happiness. It would be wiser and better, on the belief of an endless life, to seek, by an obedience to all the laws of God written in our physical, moral, and spiritual natures, to escape from all misery in a world where no sin or sorrow can ever enter.

The future punishment threatened in Scripture, is not

TORMENT IN LITERAL FIRE.

The belief has been, and is still entertained by many, that the wicked will be tormented in literal fire in hell forever. But is this the meaning of those Scriptures, which represent hell as a place of fire? Can it, in any way, be definitely ascertained what is meant, when we read of the lake that burneth with fire and brimstone? We think it can. Some have discouraged all inquiry on this point, as though it were profane and presumptuous. But I see not why we are not bound to investigate the import of God's Word here as elsewhere. The Holy One certainly did not intend to deceive us, or to move us to obedience by untruth. He meant that we should know just what he intended to reveal. It is for us to search, to know the mind of the spirit. A diligent comparison of the various Scriptural representations of future punishment, and a careful consideration of the symbolic nature of fire, as employed in the Word of God, will show definitely what is and what is not meant.

SYMBOLIC IMPORT OF FIRE.

It is common among the sacred writers, in denouncing the judgments of God against the guilty, to employ the destructive agents in the material world as symbols of agents in the moral world, which produce sufferings and ruin of a very different character from the effects of the natural agents.

This is especially true in regard to fire. The destructive energies of this element, and the torment it inflicts upon living beings, renders it an exceedingly appropriate symbol of whatever consumes, or does damage, and of all severe trials, vexations and misfortunes.

1. "*It is used as a symbol of sin, and the misery and moral ruin it produces. Prov.* 16 : 29, "An ungodly man diggeth up evil: and in his lips there is a *burning fire.*" Here the words of an ungodly man—the scoffs and slanders—the blasphemies, and lies, and bitter words which proceed from his lips, are said to be *a fire*, on account of the mischief, and misery, and ruin they effect. *Isaiah* 9 : 18, "For wickedness burneth as the fire; it shall devour the briers and thorns, and shall kindle in the thickets of the forest, and they shall mount up like the lifting up of smoke." Wickedness does immense injury in the world. It is productive of incalculable misery, and hence it is here compared to a fire kindled amid briers and thorns, and in the thickets of the forest, furiously spreading its wasting flame wide and desolating on every hand, and lifting up its column of smoke as a burning furnace to heaven. Such is sin, in its destructive and misery-working consequences in the estimation of God.

2. Fire is very extensively employed in Scripture as a symbol of those severe trials and afflic-

tions, and desolating judgments which God, in the ordinary or extraordinary operations of his providence, brings upon individuals and nations for their sins. Only a few of the more prominent passages can be noticed.

Zach. 13 : 9, "And I will bring the third part through the fire, and will refine them as silver is refined, and will try them as gold is tried." *Is.* 48 : 10, "Behold I have refined thee, but not with silver; I have chosen thee in the *furnace* of affliction." *Ps.* 66 : 12, "Thou hast caused men to ride over our heads; we went through *fire* and through water: but thou broughtest us out into a wealthy place."

The meaning of these Scriptures obviously is, that God led his people through great and severe trials and afflictions on account of sin before effecting for them the deliverances recorded.

The judgments brought upon the Jews for their great iniquities, by wars, pestilence, famine, and dispersion among the nations, with the untold calamities that followed them, are repeatedly threatened under the symbol of a burning furnace of fire.

Ezekiel, 22 : 13–15 and 18–22, "Behold, therefore, I have smitten mine hand at thy dishonest gain which thou hast made, and at thy blood which has been in the midst of thee. Can thy heart endure, or can thy hands be strong, in the days that I shall deal with thee? I, the Lord, have spoken it, and will do it. And I will scatter thee among heathen, and disperse thee in the countries, and will *consume* thy filthiness out of thee."

"Son of man, the house of Israel is to me become dross: all they are brass, and tin, and iron, and lead, in the midst of the furnace: they are even the dross of silver. Therefore, thus saith the Lord God, because ye are all become dross, behold, therefore, I will gather you in the midst of Jerusalem. As they gather silver, and brass, and iron, and lead, and tin, into the midst of the furnace, to blow the *fire* upon it, to melt it; so will I gather you in mine anger and in my fury, and I will leave you there and *melt* you. Yea, I will gather you, and blow upon you in the *fire* of my wrath, and ye shall be *melted* in the midst thereof. As silver is melted in the midst of the furnace, so shall ye be melted in the midst thereof; and ye shall know that I, the Lord, have poured out my fury upon you."

History informs us how these fearful threatenings were fulfilled; not by literal fire; but by famine, and pestilence, and war, and captivity, and those terrible sufferings which followed their dispersion and bondage.

These evils, therefore, which came upon them, on account of their iniquities, when abandoned of God, were altogether of a different character from those produced by fire. Fire as an agent is put for analogous agents, and its destructive effects in the production of misery and ruin for those analogous effects produced by famine, pestilence and war. And in this case the appropriateness and significance of the symbolic emblem is clearly seen.

The full and entire destruction of the Assyrian Empire is predicted by *Isaiah* under the symbol of a fierce burning fire which consumes it in all its parts.

For its pride, and especially its oppression of the people of God, the prophet was commanded to prophesy against it, saying, "Therefore shall the Lord of hosts send among his fat ones leanness; and under his glory he shall *kindle a burning like the burning of a fire.* And the light of Israel shall be for a fire, and his holy One for a flame, and it shall burn and devour his thorns and his briers in one day; and shall consume the glory of his forests, and of his fruitful fields, both soul and body, and they shall be as when a standard-bearer fainteth."

Assyria has long since been destroyed. The destruction predicted has come upon her to the uttermost. We now look for her in vain among the nations of the earth. The besom of annihilation has swept over her, and left not a trace of her ancient grandeur and glory, except as they are now dug up from the mouldering dust of her rock-carved monuments. From history we learn that it was not by fire merely, but by war and conquest, and all the desolations which commonly attended Oriental warfare, that she was consumed.

No agent in nature could more appropriately be used, as a symbol to represent the wide and ruinous destructions which came upon her, than fire, which possesses a most tormenting power, and consumes with irresistible energy, all that is combustible before it.

The destruction of Idumea, also, for its cruelties, oppressions, and pride, as seen in the perpetual desolations which now reign over all her cities and towns, and territories, were foretold, among other representations, under the symbol of fire, and her perpetual desolations as a smoke that ascendeth up forever and ever. *Is.* 34: 5, 6, 8, 9, 10. "For my sword shall be bathed in heaven: behold it shall come down upon Idumea, and upon the people of my curse, to judgment. The sword of the Lord is filled with blood, it is made fat with fatness, and with the blood of lambs and goats, with the fat of the kidneys of rams; for the Lord hath a sacrifice in Bozrah, and a great slaughter in the land of Idumea. For it is the day of the Lord's vengeance, and the year of the recompenses for the controversy of Zion. And the streams thereof shall become *burning pitch.* It shall not be quenched night nor day; the smoke thereof shall go up forever: from generation to generation it shall lie waste: none shall pass through it forever and ever."

Idumea has been destroyed. The sacrifice has been made in Bozrah, and the desolations foretold have came upon her. Travellers attest, that over all her cities, towns, and country, reigns one wild and irreclaimable waste. The prophecy has been most signally and terribly fulfilled. But Idumea was not destroyed by fire. Her streams were not all literally turned into pitch, nor her dust into brimstone; nor is there any literal smoke now seen ascending up from the fires that have been kindled upon her. Other

Scriptures show that it was principally by invasion and war, and all the carnage and upheavings commonly consequent upon them, that she was made a perpetual desolation. But God's word is true, in the sense and form intended.

The pitch, and the brimstone, and the fire, and the smoke ascending perpetually, were symbols of analogous agents, and effects analogous to the effects of fire, which were to exert their fury and force upon her.

The figure of a great burning, sending up its dense smoke continually, is a most expressive representation of those desolating effects which there continually prevail.

The overthrow of ancient Babylon, too, effected by the conquests of the Medo-Persian kings, and subsequent wars, was foretold by *Isaiah*, chap. 47: 14, under the symbol of a burning fire.

In all these enumerated cases, it is seen that fire, on account of its destructive energy as a fearful agent in nature, and its power to produce misery, is employed as an emblem or symbol of corresponding destructions produced by entirely different agents, as punishments for sin.

Now the force of the argument drawn from these examples of the symbolic use of fire, in reference to the future punishments of the wicked, is this—as fire, on account of its destructive energy, and its power to produce misery, is very generally employed in Scripture, as a symbol to represent all the great, varied, and terrible calamities which in the providence of God came upon men as the fruit or punishment of sin; so, according to the analogies of the word of God, when fire is spoken of in reference to the eternal torment of the wicked, it is still used as a symbol simply of those miseries they will suffer in consequence of sin, of whatever nature they may be.

To us there is great force in this argument, as it rests not on human authority or opinion, but upon the exposition which God has given of his own word. It is very common in Scripture, to represent one kind of punishment, or misery, by the effects produced by some destructive agent in nature, whose literal effects are of altogether a different kind. But the connection in which the figure is employed, and the nature of the subject, will uniformly show in what sense symbols are used.

The above conclusion is sustained by a reference to, and a careful examination of, those passages in the Old and New Testament, which directly represent the future punishment of the wicked under the symbol or emblem of fire.

There are various passages in the book of Revelations, which are often quoted in proof of eternal punishment, and which are supposed by many to teach the existence of some place or lake of literal fire and brimstone in which the wicked will be tormented forever; but a careful examination of these passages will show that no such thing can be meant, or was ever intended. The book of Revelations is manifestly a symbolical book throughout, and cannot be consistently understood, except expounded according to some regular and well-established law of symbolization. But if we explain the greater part symbolically, consistency requires that we should the remainder, and this renders it necessary for us to understand the phrase "Lake of fire and brimstone" in a symbolic, and not in a literal sense.

The first passage we will notice is found in chapter 19: 20, 21, "And the beast was taken, and with him the false prophet that wrought miracles before him, with which he deceived them that had received the mark of the beast, and them that worshipped his image. *These both were cast alive into a lake of fire* burning with brimstone. And the remnant were slain with the sword of him that sat upon the horse, which sword proceeded out of his mouth: and all the fowls were filled with their flesh."

In the prophecy, of which these words are a part, the downfall and destruction of the great mystic Babylon, with confederated nations, is foretold. Now, it is manifest, that their being cast into a lake of fire, burning with brimstone, cannot be understood in a literal sense, from the fact, that the beast and false prophet cast into it, are not two persons or individuals, but great legalized anti-christian confederacies, which, in opposition to the true church, have spread over ages, and through successive generations, and which have no existence, except in the present world. National sins, or anti-christian confederacies, can only exist and be punished in the present world. In the future we must appear as individuals, and as such be rewarded or punished. It would be impossible to cast the beast and the false prophet, who symbolically represent a long line of rulers, or long successive generations of anti-christian confederacies, into a literal lake of fire and brimstone.

In harmony with the uniform representations of Scripture, the fire and brimstone here are symbolical of those severe and righteous judgments which in the present world are yet to come upon those represented by the beast and the false prophet, for their destruction, by whatever means accomplished, and their being cast into this lake of fire, signifies their entire and eternal destruction from earth.

This exposition is confirmed by a reference to the passage found in chapter 20 : 14. In summoning up the results of the judgments of God, and the consummation of the great day, the Revelator says, "And death and hell, or Hades, were cast into the lake of fire. This is the second death. "And whosoever was not found written in the book of life was cast into the lake of fire."

But how could death, a mere imaginary, personified agent, and Hades, the invisible state—an abode or place merely of the dead, be cast into a literal lake of material fire? There is no such real being in the universe as death. Death is a fact, or an event, which occurs to all the living of earth, by the decree and agency of God. But in figurative language, it is very properly represented as a monster of sin—a cruel resistless tyrant, and Hades that invisible world, or the grave, to which death assigns all whom he destroys. Their being cast into the lake of fire, signifies simply their entire destruction from earth. They are here to have no more place or power after the period designated. When all the dead are raised to life, and every individual redeemed from the power of the grave, then indeed death and Hades will be destroyed from earth effectually, and forever. And what could more appropriately represent the eternal destruction of these long-dreaded enemies of the human race, than to represent them as cast into a lake of fire burning with brimstone?

In the two cases now noticed, the import of being cast into the lake of fire is clearly defined by the very nature and necessities of the case. Why not, then, give this clearly-defined, and consistent import, to all the other passages in this book in which the same lake of fire is mentioned? In connection with the destruction of death and Hades, symbolized by their being cast into a lake of fire, it is said, "And the devil that deceived them was cast into the lake of fire and brimstone, where the beast and the false prophet are, and shall be tormented day and night forever and ever. And whosoever was not found written in the Book of Life was cast into the lake of fire." Now, as the casting of the beast and the false prophet, and of death and Hades into the lake of fire, signifies simply their destruction from earth, so the casting of the devil, and of those who are not written in the Book of Life, into the lake of fire, symbolically represents their destruction from earth also. The devil is yet to be banished or destroyed from earth, and all the wicked; for, says the apostle, those who obey not the gospel, "shall be punished with everlasting destruction from the presence of the Lord and from the glory of his power."

The fact here stated in respect to the devil, that he shall be tormented day and night forever and ever, and of other wicked, in chapter 14 : 11, that the smoke of their torment ascendeth up forever and ever, clearly indicates that their destruction from earth will not be annihilation, but a perpetuity of misery of a nature hereafter to be explained.

In the case of Idumea, already noticed, *Is.* 34 : 10, her perpetual desolations are symbolically represented by a smoke going up forever and ever. But there is no fire or smoke there. It is a most striking and significant symbol of perpetuity of destruction. So in the case before us, the fire and the smoke going up forever and ever, only represent the perpetuity of that destruction and misery they suffer. There is, therefore, just as much evidence that there is a literal fire and smoke in Idumea, as there is or will be in hell.

LITERAL FIRE NOT INTENDED BY CHRIST.

The various representations of our Lord respecting the future punishment of the wicked, are supposed by some, to teach the existence of literal, material fire in hell.

The parable of Dives and Lazarus is relied upon for this purpose. This Scripture is too familiar to need quotation in full. "The rich man died, and was buried, and in hell he lifted up his eyes being in torment, and seeing Abraham afar off and Lazarus in his bosom, he cried, saying, Father Abraham send Lazarus that he may dip the tip of his finger in water to cool my tongue, for I am tormented in this *flame.*"

Now, there are some facts here brought to view which conclusively show that no literal fire can possibly be meant, and that the whole must be a parable designed to illustrate some important truths of which it is not our object now to speak. The body of Dives, we are assured, was buried in the grave. It was only his soul then, his spiritual, immaterial part, that was conscious in hell. He therefore had no material body, at the time, that could be tormented in material fire, and no tongue that could be cooled with water. The body of Lazarus was also in the grave. His soul only was in paradise, and he had, therefore, no material finger to dip in water. These facts, definitely stated in the account, show that the descriptions given cannot be literal. For, if taken in any literal sense, it would require us to believe that Lazarus could dip a spiritual finger in material water and cool a spiritual tongue. Would not this be making the Scriptures teach absurdity and nonsense?

Our Lord, in *Mark*, 9 : 43–48, and other places, represents those who enter not into life, as being cast at last into hell, into the fire that shall never be quenched: where the worm dieth not, and the fire is not quenched. The figure in these passages is taken from the valley of Hinnom, near Jerusalem, where in ancient times the bloody rites of Moloch were performed, and children offered in sacrifice. To render this place execrable and an abomination, it was made, during the reign of the pious kings of Judah, the common sewer of Jerusalem, in which all the filth and dead bodies of animals were cast, and where, consequently, the worm or maggots were never absent, and where fires were kept continually burning, to consume the filth there deposited. In process of time, this most dismal and loathsome place of corruption and death, was employed as a symbol or representation of that dark world, where the corruption of sin only will reign, and where the misery resulting therefrom will be eternal. And a most expressive and fearful figure it is. But there is one fact here stated, which shows that our Lord, in making use of this valley of Hinnom as a representation of hell, did not mean to teach the existence there of literal fire. He says. that there the *worm will not die*, as well as that the fire will not be quenched. Now, if these passages teach that hell is a place of literal fire, they also as clearly and emphatically teach that there is a literal worm, or maggots there, *which will live forever*, and revel among the lost.

But who can believe such absurdity as this? Many of the Latin fathers, we are told, did not shrink from advocating an opinion so revolting. Most modern commentators, however, make the worm to signify the conscience of the guilty, which will be an eternal tormenter. Supposing, then, that the worm denotes the conscience, or remorse, or despair, or something in the mind itself, and not external, then consistency requires us to understand the fire as representing some cause of torment in the mind also—the depraved passions of the lost which will burn as a fire, and rage continually.

In *Matt.* 25 : 46, our Lord is represented as saying, "Depart from me, ye cursed, into everlasting fire prepared for the devil and his angels." But it is clear that literal, material fire cannot here be meant; for, as the devil and his angels are spirits, and possess not material natures like ourselves, as we know of, the fire prepared for them must be something very different from literal fire. It will be, we doubt not, the fire of sin, and its torment will be the torment resulting from their own depraved natures, shut up and confined within those limits which God will set to their dreary prison-house.

Jude says, that Sodom and Gomorrah, and the cities about them, for their wickedness, "are set forth for an example, suffering the vengeance of *eternal fire.*" But the inhabitants of Sodom and Gomorrah are now disembodied spirits, and cannot, therefore, be suffering the vengeance of material fire. The meaning of this passage seems clearly to be this: the effects of the fires which consumed them are perpetual, in and about the Dead Sea. In the fires which consumed them, therefore, and which are denominated eternal, on account of their lasting effects, they are set forth as an example of warning to all other similar transgressors.

INCONSISTENT WITH DEGREES IN PUNISHMENT.

In connection with the argument above presented, against the idea of a punishment inflicted by literal fire in hell, drawn from the very common symbolic use of fire in Scripture, we derive another, from all those passages which declare that, in a future world, God will render to every man according to his works. There is no principle of Divine government declared more fully or clearly in Scripture than this, and none could be more equitable or just. But would not this principle be most manifestly violated, were all the condemned indiscriminately to be cast into a lake of literal fire, and there tormented forever? Would not this be punishing all alike? Would this be rendering to each according to the deeds done in the body? If the benighted heathen, and the accomplished sinner in Zion—if those who have lived under a darker dispensation, in common with those who have continued in sin under the clear light of the gospel, are alike and eternally to be tormented in the same lake of fire, what becomes of the declaration of our Lord, that it shall be more tolerable for the heathen in the day of judgment than for the gospel sinner? To make hell a place of material fire, is certainly to bring these various Scriptures into direct collision. But if we suppose that the simple punishment of sin will be the abandonment of the sinner by God, to himself in hell, to suffer the legitimate consequences of his own sins, to eat the fruit of his own doings, then the degrees of punishment must vary, as infinitely as do the characters and sins of men in their diversified shades and aggravations. It would seem that this consideration alone must compel us to understand all those Scriptures which speak of fire, in connection with punishment, in a figurative or symbolic sense.

INCONSISTENT WITH OTHER SCRIPTURES.

Another argument against the doctrine under consideration, is derived from the fact that the various Scriptural representations respecting the place of future punishment, and the kinds of punishment inflicted, are wholly irreconcilable with the idea of literal and eternal torment in fire.

The abode of the wicked in a future world is represented as a lake of fire. *Rev.* 20: 12. As a pit that has no bottom. *Rev.* 20: 3. As a great and deep valley, where not only fires burn, but where worms continually revel. *Mark*, 9: 44. As a place separated from paradise only by a deep, impassable ravine. *Luke*, 16: 26. As a place of outer darkness. *Matthew*, 8: 12. As a prison. *Matthew*, 5: 25.

Now, some of these must be metaphorical or symbolical; for not without the greatest confusion and contradiction of ideas can it be believed, that hell can at the same time be a lake, burning with fire and brimstone, and yet a deep valley, filled with worms that never die—a lake and a valley, and yet a bottomless pit, and still in addition to these, a great prison-house, and a place of outer darkness! And yet the principle of interpretation which would lead us to believe that hell is a place of literal fire, would compel us to take all these representations as literal, and thus the Scriptures would be made to teach impossibilities.

As the place of punishment is presented under various names, so are the punishments as variously denominated. They are represented as the torment produced by fire—as the weeping and wailing, and gnashing of teeth, produced by the disappointment of being shut out from a marriage feast—as being beaten with stripes—as delivered over to tormentors, and still more frequently as reaping only the fruit of that which has been sown. As it is impossible that all these representations should be literally true, it is necessary that we should understand them in a parabolic, metaphorical, or symbolical sense. So regarding them, they carry a meaning consistent and harmonious, as a variety of figures may appropriately be employed to represent and illustrate the bitter effects of sin.

Having now, in accordance with the plan proposed, considered some of those things which do not constitute the future punishment of the wicked, we will proceed to inquire, in the light of Scripture, in what it does consist?

It may aid us in comprehending this subject to bear in mind, that, according to Scripture,

HELL IS A PLACE.

All created beings are limited. They cannot be omnipresent, and must consequently occupy some definite place. They cannot be here, and there, and everywhere at the same time. This will be as true in the world to come, as it is now.

Now, we are told, in the word of God, that the wicked shall not stand in his sight, nor sinners in the congregation of the righteous. Among the saints "there shall in no wise enter anything that defileth, neither whatsoever worketh abomination, or maketh a lie."—Rev. 21 : 27. No truth is more clearly presented in Scripture, than that there is to be a complete and an eternal separation between the righteous and the wicked in the world to come. If so, then the wicked must all be in some world or place by themselves. They are to be punished with everlasting destruction, *away* from the presence of God, and the glorious manifestations of his power. This place is represented as an outer darkness, some place outside the light of heaven's glory, removed far beyond the region of the pure and good. It is a prison, in which the guilty of the universe will be confined, and prevented from doing further injury, just as we shut those up now in our prisons who are unfit for society abroad. To this place or prison the wicked will be sentenced, and doomed by the judgment of God, and the approbation of all the good, because they are unfitted for the society of the holy, and would mar the happiness of heaven were they there.

PUNISHMENT THE CONSEQUENCE OF SIN.

Cast out into this receptacle of sin, one peculiar part, and perhaps the greater and most terrible of their punishment will consist in being forsaken of God, in some peculiar manner, and left to themselves, to eat of their own ways, and to reap the natural and necessary results of their own conduct. That the wicked will be forsaken of God is clearly implied in all those Scriptures which declare that they shall *depart from him*, that they shall be *driven* away—that they shall be punished *from his presence*, and from the glory of his power. God often leaves wicked men in this world without his protection, to go on in their own way, and to bring upon themselves the miserable results of their own evil doings. Will it be unjust or unkind for him to do the same to those hereafter, who do not love him, and who do not will that he should reign over them?

The Scriptures are abundant in declaring that the peculiar punishment of sin will be the fruit of sin itself, when the sinner is forsaken of God, and left to his own ways. The following passages, quoted in the order in which they occur in the Word, fully confirm this important truth:

Job, 4 : 8, "Even as I have seen, they that plough iniquity and sow wickedness *reap the same.*" *Prov.* 1 : 31, "Therefore shall they *eat* of the *fruit* of their own way, and be *filled with their own devices.*" *Isaiah*, 3 : 11, "Wo unto the wicked! it shall be ill with him: *for the reward of his hands shall be given him.*" 9 : 18, "For *wickedness burneth as the fire.*" *Jer.* 2 : 19, "*Thine own wickedness* shall correct thee, and thy backslidings shall reprove thee: know, therefore, and see that it is an evil thing and bitter, that thou hast forsaken the Lord thy God, and that my fear is not in thee, saith the Lord God of hosts." *Hos.* 8 : 7, "For they have sown the wind, and they shall reap the whirlwind." 10 : 13, "Ye have ploughed wickedness, ye have *reaped iniquity;* ye have eaten the fruit of lies."

Gal. 6 : 7, 8, "Be not deceived; God is not mocked; for *whatsoever* a man soweth *that* shall he also reap. For he that soweth to his flesh shall of the flesh reap corruption: but he that soweth to the Spirit, shall of the Spirit reap life everlasting."

These Scriptures, with many others of similar import, which might be quoted, clearly teach that the peculiar punishment of sin will be the fruit—the natural and legitimate effect of wickedness developing and producing its own misery. As in the natural world, men gather the kind of grain they sow, and generally in proportion as they sow and cultivate it; so in the world to come, every man will gather or reap that which he has sown.

This is fully confirmed, and may more clearly appear, from a consideration of the peculiar penalty of the law threatened against sin. Thus it is written, "*The wages of sin is death.*"—*Rom.* 6 : 23. "*The soul that sinneth it shall die.*"—*Ez.* 18 : 20. "Turn ye, turn ye from your evil ways; for why will ye die?" 33 : 11. This is doubtless the second death, of which being cast into the lake of fire is a symbol. But what is that death, which constitutes the wages of sin? Can we, in any way, determine what it means? It is doubtless a figure drawn from natural death, for the purpose of more clearly illustrating its fearful nature to the comprehension of man. The figure must be founded on some obvious analogy between the two, and by tracing out this analogy in the light of nature and Scripture, we may learn definitely what is meant.

The most obvious and natural idea of death is, *separation.* It is not an annihilation, or a total extinction of being; but a *dissolution*, or separation of the different elements of our being. When a man dies there is a separation of soul and body. "Then shall the dust return to the earth as it was, and the spirit shall return to God who gave it." This dissolution of the union between soul and body is death. Separation is the great idea involved. Nor does the separation end in the dissolution of soul and body. In the grave the body is dissolved into its original elements. A separation takes place between all the substances of which it is composed, until it is all dissipated and gone from human view.

Thus, death is seen to be, at every step of its progress, a dissolution, or separation; and it is on this account, we doubt not, that the fruits and effects of sin are denominated death.

Sin does now, and will in the world to come, produce a separation between the sinner and God, the sinner and heaven, the sinner and the sinless, the sinner and holiness, the sinner and that eternal life of blessedness which is in reserve for the pure, analogous to that separation which takes place at death between soul and body, and between the dying and all the beauties of earth, and the attractions and enjoyments of life.

As a separation, therefore, is the great idea involved in natural death, so a separation is the great idea involved in that second death which is the effect and fruit of sin, and the one may very appropriately be employed as a figure or representation of the other.

Now, it may be distinctly seen, that in every aspect of that separation which constitutes the death of sin, it is produced directly by *sin itself*, and not by any merely arbitrary infliction of punishment by the Holy One. The Scriptures are abundant in declaring, that one prominent part of the punishment of sin will consist in an *eternal separation* of the wicked from the blissful smiles and enjoyment of God in heaven, and the society and blessedness of the holy. "The wicked shall not stand in his sight, nor sinners in the congregation of the righteous," *Ps.* 1; and at the last the Judge will say, "Depart from me ye cursed," "Depart from me ye workers of iniquity." And those who love not God and obey not the Gospel, "shall be punished with everlasting destruction from his presence and the glory of his power."—2 *Thess.* 1 : 9. Here, then, is a separation—a death declared, and one too which will take place according to an inevitable law of God's moral universe—a law which we see in operation all around us, and which cannot be avoided without remodelling and revolutionizing the whole scheme of natural and moral being. Do we not see, that where there is a dislike of one individual to another, it will separate and drive them apart? That where there is no true affection, no congeniality of character and feeling, there must and will be separation, when natural laws are left to operate without obstruction?

"How can two walk together, except they be agreed?" Just as certainly, therefore, as the pure on earth are disposed to separate from the impure by a natural law of being, just as surely as the serious have no true love for the society of the trifling and vain, and would gladly separate from them if they could, just as naturally as the refined seek other society for their association and enjoyment, than the sensual and vulgar—so by an inevitable and natural law will sin, when it is finished, bring forth death, and separate the sinner eternally from God and the holy, and from their blessedness. "Your sins," says the prophet, "have separated between you and your God, and your iniquities have hid his face from you."

They who love not God, and who love not his service, and prefer not, above every other, the society of the holy, could not be happy with God, and in such associations, were they admitted to heaven. That state of mind which excludes many from the services of the sanctuary on earth, and which renders so many indifferent to the commands of God, and the claims of the Gospel, would were there a back or open door in heaven, cause them to break company with its society and its God, and to separate themselves from services in which they had no heart, and which must therefore be an eternal weariness. It will not, then, be an exertion of Almighty power merely, which by dint of physical and irresistible energy, will take up the sinner, and hurl him headlong down to hell, whether he will or not; but it will be the result of a moral repulsion. It will be sin—his own corrupt—his own cherished wicked character, which will separate between him and his God, and drive him away to the abode of kindred spirits.

We are assured in Scripture that this great law of moral being—of affinities and repulsions, which we now see operating in all the arrangements of life, though broken and distorted by counteracting influences, will be perfectly developed in the life to come. Here every man will find his level, and his place, and there will be no such commingling of heterogeneous elements as are seen in the moral chaos of the present world. Heaven will attract its own, and draw with a more than magnetic power all that love God to his throne. And hell, too, will draw to its dark and impure dominions all whom heaven owns not on account of sin. All will go to *their own place*, as did Judas—the place for which their characters, as they respect God and his laws, will fit them. We can all see that this must and will be the fruit of sin.

And then, too, the death of the wicked in respect to their separation from happiness or their eternal misery, will be also the effect of sin, according to an established and necessary law of God in his government of moral beings. It is written in his word, and in the experience of the human mind, that where there is conscious guilt, there must be torment. There is an indissoluble connection between the two. The one follows in the train of the other, as necessarily as any effect follows its cause. And hence a consciousness of guilt will inevitably separate the sinner from happiness, let his dwelling be where it may. The great idea, then, involved in that death, which is the wages of sin, is in strict accordance with those Scriptures, which teach that the misery of the lost will be peculiarly and preeminently the fruit of their own doings. And as these point out definitely the nature of future punishment, we are justified in expounding the various figurative and symbolic representations of the Bible in harmony with them.

SIN CAN PRODUCE INTENSE MISERY.

The view now taken is not contradicted by the fact that there will be great misery in hell; for there is a power in sin to produce torment indescribable, which is appropriately shadowed forth in the worm that never dies, and in the fires that will never be quenched. Many cases have occurred in the present world which show that terrible sufferings may be endured from the natural and legitimate operations of a depraved and unsanctified mind, abandoned of God—upon which unholy passions, remorse, and despair, are suffered to work their results unrestrained.

According to Scripture, one of the heaviest woes that can fall upon a creature is to be forsaken of God. Written for our admonition are such warnings as the following, *Hos.* 9 : 12, "Yea, woe also to them when I *depart* from them!" 5 : 5, 6, "And the pride of Israel doth testify to his face; therefore, shall Israel and Ephraim fall in their iniquity; Judah also shall fall with them. They shall go with their flocks and with their herds to seek the Lord; but they shall not find him; *he hath withdrawn himself from them.*"

The deep degradation and misery of the heathen world described by the apostle in the first chapter of Romans, are ascribed to their own wickednesss when forsaken, or abandoned of God. On account of their idolatries and abominable deeds, it is said, "Wherefore God gave them up to uncleanness, through the lusts of their own hearts, to dishonor their own bodies between themselves: who changed the truth of God into a lie, and worshipped and served the creature *more than* the Creator, who is blesssed forever. *For this cause God gave them up unto vile affections.* And even as *they did not like to retain God* in their knowledge, *God gave them over to a reprobate mind*, to do those things which are not convenient: Being filled with all unrighteousness, fornication, wickedness, covetousness, maliciousness, full of envy, murder, debate, deceit, malignity; whisperers, backbiters, haters of God, despiteful, proud, boasters, inventors of evil things, disobedient to parents, without understanding, covenant-breakers, without natural affection, implacable, unmerciful: Who knowing the judgment of God, that they which commit such things are *worthy of death*," that is, of eternal separation from him, "not only do the same, but have pleasure in them that do them." *Deut.* 31 : 17. "Then my anger shall be kindled against them in that day, and I will *forsake them*, and I will *hide my face* from them, and they shall be devoured, and many evils and troubles shall befall them, so that they will say in that day, Are not these evils come upon us, *because our God is not among us?* And I will surely hide my face in that day, for all the evils which they shall have wrought, in that they are turned unto other Gods."

From these Scriptures, it is manifest that to be forsaken of God, and left to the consequences of sin, is the most fearful evil threatened in Scripture. Such an abandonment is followed by a downward course of wickedness, and by evils and miseries even in this life most appalling. And yet we have seen that it takes place according to a natural and necessary law of God's moral universe. And as a matter of simple justice, who cannot see its entire equity? If men forsake God, and desire not that he should rule over them, and refuse to obey his commands, and practice the things that he has forbidden them, and persevere in sin, is it wrong that he should give them up to do as they will, and reap the bitter fruits of their doings? "Shall not the Judge of all the earth do right?" And yet we are assured that he has often forsaken men and abandoned them to their own ways,—that he does it now, and will do it in the world to come. All through the Word, we are warned that this separation must and will be the result of sin.

And from facts revealed in Scripture and human experience, we have reason to infer that an abandonment of God will be followed by anguish most terrible and insupportable. The Lord Jesus Christ, suffered in the stead of sinners. He bore our sins in his own body on the tree. In some mysterious manner, which we may hope better to understand in another life, he endured the curse of the law—

that death or separation from God which is the peculiar penalty of sin. He endured without a murmur or complaint, the cruel mockings and scourgings of his enemies, and his merely physical agonies on the cross, did not produce a recorded groan; but under the agony of mind produced by being forsaken of God, He cried out, *My God! my God! why hast thou forsaken me?* Mysterious cries! mysterious sufferings! O my soul, listen, and learn what it is, or will be, to be forsaken of God! Sinner, come to the cross of Jesus, and listen, and inquire, Can my heart endure, or can my hands be strong in the day, when God shall thus leave me? Well might the evangelist ask, "If they do these things in a green tree, what shall be done in the dry?" *Luke*, 23 : 31. That is, if an innocent being suffered such intense agony, when the Father left him, what may not the guilty suffer, when God departs forever from them?

Saul, king of Israel, was forsaken of God, on account of his wickedness, and the consequences developed in this life were, that in sore dismay and distress he betook himself to a reputed witch for information, and then in despair committed suicide. 1 *Sam.* 28 : 15, 31 : 4. The Jews, when forsaken of God, in the final overthrow of their city, raved against and devoured each other like maddened wild beasts, and were consumed in unutterable terrors.

Who has not read the affecting account of the death of the noble Altamont, given by Dr. Young?

He felt and knew that he was forsaken of God, on account of his blasphemies and gross impieties. Among other things he said to a friend, whom he had seduced to sin, "My much injured friend! my soul, as my body, lies in ruins—in scattered fragments of broken thought: remorse for the past throws my thoughts on the future. Worse dread of the future, strikes it back on the past. I turn and turn, and find no ray of light. Didst thou feel the mountain that is on me, thou wouldst struggle with the martyr for his stake, and bless heaven for the flames." A little after, he cried out, "My principles have poisoned my friend; my extravagance has beggared my boy; my unkindness has murdered my wife! And is there another hell? Oh! thou blasphemed, yet most indulgent Lord God! Hell is a refuge if it hides me from thy power." All this mental agony was only the effect of sin. God had left him justly, as a warning to others, to taste this side the grave the bitterness of forsaking God, and thus rendering it necessary, according to his laws, that he should be forsaken.

Francis Newport was an apostate from religion, and for years gave himself up to the greatest irregularities and excesses in sinful indulgence. It is said, that "a few days before his death, the violence of his torments were such, that he sweat in the most prodigious manner." At one time, looking towards the fire, he said, "Oh! that I was to lie and broil upon the fire for a hundred thousand years, to purchase the favor of God, and to be reconciled to him again! But it is a fruitless, vain wish; millions of millions of years will bring me no nearer the end of my tortures than one poor hour. O Eternity! Eternity! who can properly paraphrase upon the words forever and ever?" And then, with his last breath, he exclaimed, "Oh! the unsufferable pangs of hell and damnation."

In all this inward torment, and this fearful looking for of judgment, there was no disturbing element but sin. This was the worm that reveled within, and this the fire that could not be quenched. And now just add eternity to all, let this misery run on forever, and it would furnish an amount of wretchedness sufficiently aggravated to answer all the fearful delineations of the Word of God. There is no human tongue can tell the misery which simple remorse may produce. Mr. Garland, in his published life of John Randolph, has given a most affecting account of his death-bed scene. He says, "For a short time before he died, he lay perfectly quiet, with his eyes closed. He suddenly roused up, and exclaimed, '*Remorse! Remorse! Remorse!*' It was thrice repeated—the last time at the top of his voice, with great agitation. He cried out, 'Let me see the word. Get a dictionary.' 'There is none in the room, sir.' 'Write it down, then,—let me see the word.' The doctor picked up one of his cards, upon which was printed, Randolph, of Roanoke. 'Shall I write it on this card?' 'Yes,' he replied; 'nothing more proper.' The word Remorse was then written in pencil. He took the card in a hurried manner, and fastening his eyes upon it with great intensity,—'Write it on the back,' he exclaimed. It was so done, and handed him again. He was extremely agitated. '*Remorse! Remorse!* he exclaimed, 'you have no idea what it is. You can form no idea of it whatever; it has contributed to bring me to my present situation. Now,' he said, 'let John take your pencil, and draw a line under the word,' which was accordingly done. 'What am I to do with the card?' inquired the doctor. 'Put it in your pocket—take care of it; when I am dead, look at it.'"

What a lesson is here furnished to the guilty! The dying statesman, in full possession of the powers of his keen mind, goaded by remorse in his last moments. And now, could we suppose that this remorse might follow him along the line of an endless life, what a dreadful doom his would be! What more would be necessary to produce the weeping and wailing and gnashing of teeth, foretold in Scripture? And yet it would all be the legitimate and necessary fruit of sin: "for wickedness burneth as the fire, it shall mount up like the lifting up of smoke." *Is.* 9 : 18.

Hell will be the abode of the wicked, and in it will rage perpetually the unholy and unrestrained passions of the lost. Let us suppose a world filled with just such as the apostle describes in his first chapter of his epistle to the Romans—those who are "Filled with all unrighteousness, fornications, wickedness, covetousness, maliciousness; full of envy, murder, debate, deceit, malignity, whisperers, backbiters, haters of God, despiteful, proud, boasters, inventors of evil things, disobedient to parents, without understanding, covenant-breakers, without natural affection, implacable, unmerciful," and what a world it would be!

All the worst passions would here exist, and rage, and reign unrestrained, except by those barriers which God might erect around the mighty prison-house, saying to their desolating waves, hitherto shalt thou come, and no further. And such a world, we are assured, hell will be—the residence and the receptacle of the Devil and his angels, and all who are associated with him in feeling and character, and who have been led captive by him at his will. And in such society, and in such a world what wickedness will exist!—what passions war and burn, what torment will sin produce in the torturings of remorse, and in the rage of malignity and despair! It will need no material fire—no positive infliction of misery, to produce all the punishment foretold in Scripture. And what figure or representation could more appropriately set forth the rage and reign of wickedness than everlasting fire—the smoke of which goeth up forever and ever.

HELL THE OPPOSITE OF HEAVEN.

Hell will doubtless be, in all its aspects, the opposite of heaven. Love will reign in heaven, envy, malignity, and hate in hell. Order will be heaven's first law—disorder will prevail in hell. Heaven will have its high festive and social enjoyments—hell will be filled with social discord and misery. Visions of God, of his glorious works, and the display of his attributes will be seen in heaven—there will be an exclusion from all these in hell. The songs of redeeming love, and the loud praises of Jehovah will thrill the souls of the holy with rapture in heaven—but wailings and blasphemies will grate harsh thunders upon the ear in hell. Heaven will present a career of upward intellectual progress unending and joyous; but intellectual darkness and degradation, will send the wicked downward to depths unmeasured. Heaven will be a society of holy beings—hell an abode of wicked spirits. As in heaven happiness will be the fruit of holiness, in conjunction with God and his glorious abode; so in hell, its misery will be the fruit of sin, in conjunction with the Devil and that outer darkness in which the impure will be involved.

As in our Father's house there are many mansions which Jesus has gone to prepare for them that love him—so in hell there may be many departments, suited to every grade of sinners, where each may receive according to his works. The self-righteous moralist, who loves not God, but himself supremely, need not fear but that he will find a place just suited to him, with enough like him to keep him company.

THE CHARACTER OF GOD VINDICATED.

According to the view of future punishment now taken, it is obvious that misery hereafter will only be a continuation of the misery produced by sin in the present world. And can any say that this is cruel or unjust? The intemperate and licentious, the dishonest and prodigal, with the wicked of divers names, often suffer in appalling forms, the degrading and bitter fruits of their conduct in the present life. Now, as God, in the laws which he has established, and in the administration of his providences, orders and suffers these things here; can it be cruel or unjust to suffer the same hereafter?

There is no way in which God can save men from sin and its consequences but by turning them from their evil ways to a new and holy life. If the wicked, therefore, will not turn and live, but enter the future world with the same character they now possess, and the same alienation from God, and vile affections, they must according to God's immutable laws continue to suffer. God has but one law, unrepealed and eternal, on this subject. The sinner must *repent* or *perish*. He must *turn*, *turn* from his evil ways if he would not die.

If any are banished to hell, and there suffer its torments, it will not be because God is unkind, unjust or cruel; but because their iniquities separate between him and them, and render them miserable.

It is the will of God that men shall not be happy, except in obedience to his laws, whether natural, moral, or physical. It is not because he delights in misery, that the wicked now suffer in consequence of violated law; but it is because he cannot bless them according to his government and character, unless they are obedient. To all transgressors, he says, "*Ye will* not come unto me that ye may have life." And this, we believe, furnishes the true solution of *eternal punishment.* The wicked will be punished eternally, because they will be sinners, unreconciled to God eternally. It will not be because God is vindictive, or revengeful, or malicious, or delights in the doom of the lost, but because pursuing an eternal and downward career of evil, they will, according to an immutable law, remain separated forever from God, and from the society and enjoyment of the holy. Did the Bible teach, and could the universalist prove that at some point in eternity, the wicked will repent, and possess new hearts, and become holy, misery would then of course cease, and, according to the law of God, that when the wicked turns from his way, he shall live, they must inevitably become happy. But the Scriptures never intimate, or assert this, and therefore it cannot be proved. It teaches that in the world to come, he that is unjust will be unjust still, and he that is filthy, will be filthy still, and he that is holy, will be holy still. *Rev.* 22.

It is often seen in this life that "evil men and seducers wax worse and worse, deceiving and being deceived," and go to such lengths in sin, that they become hardened in iniquity, and manifest no disposition in life or death to turn and live. The Word assures us, that those who turn not in this life, will go on forever in the same course, and thus forever suffer. Hence

CHRIST SAVES FROM SIN.

This view of future punishment also harmonizes most perfectly with the great salvation which Jesus Christ came into the world to provide and propose to men. Salvation, according to the Gospel, is not delivering men from hell, and placing them in heaven, merely, nor does it consist in rescuing them from some external infliction of wrath to which they are exposed; *but in saving them from sin.* "Thou shalt call his name Jesus: for he shall save his people from their sins." He gave himself for us that he might redeem us from all iniquity. Jesus of course, in seeking to save men, would aim to save them from the greatest evil to which they were exposed, and that which was comprehensive of all others. Sin is that evil. This is that abominable thing which God hates, that exceeding bitter thing which is the sinner's tormentor and misery. The salvation of Jesus, therefore, directs our attention especially to sin, as that which is most to be feared, and from which we are to escape as for our lives. To save us from this, the Holy Spirit is sent to convince of sin, to renew and sanctify the heart, and make us meet for heaven. There is no salvation revealed except from sin. If Christ came to deliver us from the wrath to come, and we are hence earnestly exhorted to flee from this wrath, it is only by turning from our evil ways, and escaping the corruptions that are in the world through lust. And all this shows that it is sin, which is the source and instrument of the wrath to come, from which we are to seek deliverance.

Now to hold up the future punishment of the wicked as consisting in misery inflicted externally to sin, and as dependent simply on the wrath and power of God, is to direct the attention of the sinner to the punishment as the great thing to be dreaded, rather than to sin itself, and its necessary and bitter consequences. Such is the aspect in which the whole subject lies in the minds of many. They are more concerned to escape hell, than they are to escape sin; more anxious to render God, in some way, propitious to them, than they are to ascend to him, and to eternal life, through the narrow way of holiness, which Jesus has opened.

But if the view of future punishment presented is Scriptural, the whole aspect of this subject is changed. Sin here is the great evil. There is nothing in the wide universe to be so much dreaded. Aside from it, there is no wrath to come, and, unredeemed from it, there is no power can save us.

And is not this in entire harmony with the whole design and tenor of the gospel. It is in accordance with the doctrine of repentance, of regeneration, of sanctification, the only and great design of which is to turn and deliver us from sin.

And it is in entire harmony, too, with that most precious and soul-cheering truth—the doctrine of justification by faith: for what is that faith in Jesus and his atonement which justifies and saves? Is it not clearly defined to be, in Scripture, a *faith* which works by love, which *purifies* the heart, and overcomes the world? A true and living faith in Christ, as presented in the gospel, cannot but give us the most convincing and appalling views of sin—and lead us to see that this is the terrible evil from which he came to save, by leading us to repentance and obedience. And besides, there is nothing but the justifying or pardoning act of God, bestowed only in connection with repentance, regeneration, and faith, that can so effectually wipe out our past sins, and destroy their misery-working power in the conscience, that they shall no longer be a source of torment. Every act of God, therefore, put forth for salvation through the Gospel, in forgiving sin, and in renewing and sanctifying the heart, as well as every duty we are called upon to perform in working out our own salvation, are in full accordance with the view taken, that sin and its own direct consequences are the great evils to be avoided. To these every effort and aim of God are directed. *And hence we do not take the first step aright in seeking salvation if we are not continually turning from sin.*

GOD THE AVENGER.

It may be thought by some that the view of future punishment presented, is contradicted by those Scriptures which represent the misery or punishment of the wicked, as inflicted by the Lord himself. "Vengeance is mine, I will repay, saith the Lord.' But there is no collision here. It is common to ascribe that to God as its author, which is produced by or in accordance with his laws. When he establishes a law, or an agency, or a course of things, designed to produce a given result, he is undoubtedly the author of the effect produced. Thus, in Scripture, God is said to provide for man and beast, in the food which is brought forth so bountifully in nature. All the blessings of life we are taught to ascribe to him, with thanksgiving, as the great Father of lights, from whom cometh down *every good and every perfect gift.* And yet it is certain that he does not bestow these bounties of providence directly, but mediately through the operation of second causes in the laws of the natural world. But God enacted all the laws and appointed all the agencies in nature, for the purpose of producing these beneficent ends for his creatures. He is therefore the author of all good, and to him all must be ascribed.

Whatever a man does designedly, by an agent, he does himself. So whatever is done by the laws or agencies of God, is to be traced up to him as the author.

On this principle it is, that God punishes sin—though punishment under the Divine government is the fruit of sin. He is the author of those laws of the human constitution according to which sin produces misery. He evidently never intended that his creatures should be prosperous and happy in disobedience to his laws. As a Being of order and purity, he seeks to propitiate their highest welfare in obedience to the laws of his government. We see this abundantly illustrated in the present world. It is only as men yield themselves obediently to the laws of nature, physical and moral, that they can expect to be long prospered and happy. The violation of any law, sooner or later brings its penalty. God made these laws, and designed their effect, and he is therefore the author of their penalty. They are inflicted by him. The intemperate man suffers, because he violates the laws of his physical nature. It is no part of the plan of the Creator that he should escape from the miserable consequences, except by turning to obedience.

On this principle it is, that the future misery of the wicked is said to be inflicted by the Lord. He created human minds, and he established the laws according to which sin or disobedience produces torment. The suffering endured is the penalty attached to sin. Though, therefore, the misery of the future world will be the direct and legitimate result of sin, as is often in the present life, it will still be a punishment inflicted by the great Judge of all.

There is hence harmony among all the works, and

laws, and various departments of the government of Jehovah. The future world will only be a continuation of the present, in which the same great laws of mind, and of happiness and misery, which operate here, will only be more perfectly carried out. In the present world, under a dispensation of grace, there are necessarily many obstructing and counteracting causes, incidental to a state of trial, to prevent the full operation of established moral laws. But in the world to come, these will not exist. Laws will take their course, upon the unsanctified, and produce their designed misery.

Some may find fault, that such laws should be established, by which men will suffer the consequences of their conduct hereafter. But they might as well complain of those arrangements in the present world according to which the guilty so often reap the fruit of their doings in disgrace and misery. But to murmur here is to contend with our Maker who does all things according to the counsels of his own will.

If it shall appear at last, that the great, wise, and good Creator could not promote the highest welfare of his universal government, and the greatest happiness of his intellgent and moral creatures, except in obedience to his laws—it will be seen that it is only a part of his goodness, as universal Lord, that the disobedient suffer. God proclaims his law through universal being—through all ranks and orders of creatures—as well as in his Word, "If ye be willing and obedient, ye shall eat the good of the land; but if ye refuse and rebel, ye shall be destroyed, and that without remedy." The obedient, therefore, have nothing to fear under the government of God—the disobedient everything. And hence it is clear that though God is the author of that constitution of things according to which the guilty suffer the just desert of their doings—

THE WICKED DESTROY THEMSELVES.

This is often affirmed in Scripture, and is implied in every command to repent, and warning to turn from sin. "O Israel, thou hast destroyed thyself." "O Israel, return unto the Lord thy God; for thou hast fallen by thine iniquity." *Prov.* 6 : 32. "But whoso committeth adultery, lacketh understanding: he that doeth it, *destroyeth his own soul.*" *Prov.* 8 : 36. "But he that sinneth against me wrongeth his own soul." *Is.* 3 : 9. "The show of their countenance doth witness against them, and they declare their sin as Sodom, they hide it not: woe unto their soul! *for they have rewarded evil unto themselves.*" *Jer.* 2 : 17. "Hast thou not procured this unto thyself, in that thou hast forsaken the Lord thy God, when he led thee by the way."

There is no contradiction between this, and the former proposition, that God is the punisher of sin. God has enacted his laws and designed their effects. If men therefore place themselves voluntarily in the way of their operation, or in opposition to them, they destroy themselves as really as they would, did they throw themselves into the fire, or into water, or on the track of a railroad, before the ponderous engine.

Fire is a creature of God. He designed its effects. If any should throw themselves into the raging element, they would be devoured, according to the appointment of the Creator, who sees it best that his laws should act uniformly; but they would be their own destroyers by disobeying the laws of God in respect to fire, and placing themselves in the way of their action. So the intemperate, the licentious, the prodigal and vicious, often bring ruin upon themselves by violating the laws of God, written in their physical and mental constitutions, and yet their suffering is the penalty which the Creator has attached to his laws, and these laws, in their effects, will operate with terrible certainty in the world to come.

In all the laws of nature and revelation, God places life and death before men, blessing and cursing; and calls upon them to choose. If they decide to violate his laws, they can do it, but in so doing, they destroy themselves. He has ordained an indissoluble connection between sin and suffering, and has appointed the laws and agents by which the penalty will most certainly be inflicted. If any, therefore, will persevere in sin, and form to themselves a wicked character, the consequences will follow, according to Heaven's appointment; but the blame will be their own. And such will be the conviction at the day of judgment. Every mouth will then be stopped.

Reader, may I not address you personally? Are you living in impenitence and sin? You hold in your hands the murderous instruments of your own self-destruction. O throw them down, ere you fatally plunge them to your own heart. You hold in your hand a cup. It is poisoned, and yet you are drinking from it. O dash it from you, ere you drink its dregs and perish! Sin may now seem pleasant. The foolish say, "stolen waters are sweet, and bread eaten in secret is pleasant." But how few reflect "that the dead are there: and that her guests are in the depths of hell." Sin, as rapidly as committed, writes itself in the moral constitution, so indelibly, that no human agency or power can erase or wash it out. Memory records it, and conscience notes it down, so that according to an immutable law, it can never be escaped.

The language of Scripture is, "For though thou wash thee with nitre, and take thee much soap, yet thine iniquity is marked before me, saith the Lord." "The sin of Judah is written with a pen of iron, and with the point of a diamond: it is graven upon the table of their heart, and upon the horns of your altars." How strongly does this language set forth the indelible nature of sin. It can never be forgotten. Its power can never be escaped, except by that repentance and faith, which lead to obedience and Jesus, for cleansing and pardon.

If you are living in sin, then, you are destroying yourself. You are placing yourself directly in the way of the straight onward movement of the laws of God, which turn not as they go, but crush all who oppose them. If you continue in sin, no power can save you; for salvation is from sin. You will be the author of your own moral ruin and misery, as much so as any guilty man is his own destroyer, who involves himself in wretchedness, in the present life, by his crimes. There is no way in the universe which leads to happiness, but the way of holiness. This is the way God has ordained, and none can disannul it. All others lead astray, and in the broad road to destruction. You may complain, you may rebel, but the holy will see that it is best for the universe, as a whole, that all the laws of God should be immutable—and hence, that the disobedient and impenitent should reap that which they have sown, and suffer the legitimate consequences of their own guilt. The immutability of the character and laws of God is the only ground of confidence to creatures. Were they not so, we should not know on what to depend. Nature might then be fickle, fire capricious in its effects, and other destructive agents in their results, and sin might or might not produce torment. And thus all would be uncertain. But we know now on what to calculate. Friend, you know. God has told you. You must obey; or if you have been disobedient, you must repent, or perish.

There is then before the guilty—

AN ALARMING PROSPECT.

Those who are unwilling to forsake their sins and to yield their unholy characters, made up of selfish and vile affections fondly cherished, may attempt to console themselves with the delusive reflection, that they will endure the consequences of their own conduct as well as they can. "But can thine heart endure, or can thine hands be strong, in the day that I shall deal with thee, saith the Lord."

We have seen that the misery produced by remorse and conscious guilt, in the present world, is often intolerable. And if sin can thus torment in a world of probation and mercy, who can tell what may be its bitter fruits in a world of retribution? There have been hours when, perhaps, you have been very sad, on account of some sin or wrong done—suppose you were destined to spend an eternity in some world of sin, in that state of mind, with no alleviation, could you endure it? Suppose, as your coffin-lid was screwed down, and you were buried, you were still conscious, and that this was to be your portion to lie there and think over the past, and the light and glory from which you were shut out,—could you endure it? And yet it may be an equally gloomy prospect, to be shut out from God and the glorious manifestations of his holiness, and left to reap the fruit of sin in a world where there will be nothing but iniquity. Any view which can be taken of the matter presents an alarming prospect.

An old writer relates, "that a vain, ungodly man was lying sleepless on his bed, and being uneasy, and finding no rest, he began to think, would any be hired to lie thus for two or three years in darkness, without friends or amusements? Would any be willing to be bound to a bed, though it were a bed of down, and never stir abroad? And he thought no one would. Then he reflected that the time would come when, willing or unwilling, he, unless snatched away by a sudden stroke, must lie upon a bed of sickness and death; and he thought, 'But what bed shall I have next, when death thrusts me out of this? What shall become of my soul in another world? Surely all men do not go to the same place after death. Do not some go one way, and some another? Is there not a hell as well as a heaven? Woe, and alas! what kind of a bed shall I find in hell? How many years shall I lie there? In what year after the first shall my misery close?' These thoughts followed him, and he could not rest. Eternity still ran in his mind. He tried to banish the solemn impression amidst gay companions and sinful delights, but in vain. Conscience, if seeming for awhile asleep, soon awoke, and inflicted fresh stings upon the soul. He thought, 'I am not certain that I shall live till to-morrow. O Eternity, if thou wert not! O Eternity, if thy place be not in heaven, though it be on a soft down bed, thou canst but be bitter and unpleasant.'"

So it is, take the mildest view of it possible, and it is terrible to think of an eternity being thus spent. But what must it be, to be wicked forever? To feel remorse and disquietude, and the rage of evil passion forever? What will it be, to be associated with the most wicked of the universe forever? Let none deceive themselves with the vain idea, that God is too good to permit these consequences of sin. *He permits them now.* Yea, he has ordained that they who violate his laws shall suffer their penalty. Do we not see this, in many cases, in the present world? Well, if these things are not inconsistent with the goodness of God in the present life, who can say that it will be unkind to permit the operation of the same great principles hereafter?

The prospect of the wicked and impenitent is indeed alarming. The idea of an eternity of misery in any form is dreadful. Suppose you were to be just as discontented, just as miserable, just as unpleasantly situated, just as unfortunate and dissatisfied in all your connections and relations as you now are forever, it would perhaps be a gloomy future for you to look to. But remember that in the world of woe all your present enjoyments and excitements will have passed away, and you will then reap unobstructed and uncounteracted the fruit of every vile affection, of every selfish disposition which you have cherished—of all the enmity to God and his laws you have manifested, and of every sin you have ever committed. And that which will give keenness to every pang, will probably be the reflection, that you have brought it all upon yourself. You, are only reaping that which you have sown.

But however alarming the prospect of the unholy in the world to come, it is rendered even more terrible by the consideration that it is—

A GREAT MYSTERY.

Whatever relates to eternal duration must be, to finite minds, an unfathomable abyss. The idea that any should be miserable forever, is indeed confounding. It is here emphatically that clouds and darkness are round about the throne of God. Who can tell what an unending eternity may evolve? O how unwilling should any be to run the risk of everlasting misery, when by repentance and faith in Jesus Christ, it may be avoided.

It is not probable that any considerations which can be presented, will ever convince the guilty and obstinately impenitent of the justice of God in their punishment. Every mouth will be stopped—but the criminal at the bar can never see his own case, as those do who are disinterested, or whose peace is to be secured by his condemnation. But there are sources of consolation to which the good may turn, even in regard to this deeply mysterious and awful subject; and considerations which are adapted to reconcile them fully to the government of God.

The character of God, as revealed, "is a refuge"—"a strong tower into which the righteous may run and be safe." He is revealed to us as infinitely holy. He will never, therefore, do anything, or suffer anything to be done in his name that is inconsistent with purity. He is a just God, and therefore no injustice or wrong can ever be done to any creature. And above all, he "*is love*," and hence we may rest assured that whatever misery the impenitent may suffer in the future world will be sanctioned by love itself. The suffering which men endure in this world, in consequence of violated law, is undoubtedly consistent with the love of God. And so it will be in the future.

The love of God is not an attribute or disposition which leads him to desire to make men happy, let them do as they will; but which seeks to bless them in accordance with his laws. His love leads him to seek to make the righteous happy—and also the wicked, by seeking to turn them from sin to the love and obedience of himself.

Human governments are benevolent when they are exercised in protecting the innocent and good, by imprisoning and punishing the guilty. So the love of God will be especially manifested in protecting the good. It will be his love to a virtuous and holy universe, which will lead him, in accordance with his laws, to cast the wicked into hell, and there leave them to eat of the fruit of their own doings. The character of God, as holy, just, and good, gives us the undoubted assurance of all this. Here we may rest in peace, believing that the Judge of all the earth will do righteously and benevolently, though his ways, to our finite minds, are now involved in deepest mystery.

Another consideration which may tend powerfully to reconcile the minds of the good, to the future misery of the wicked, is, that aside from the fallen angels, this is the only world in the universe, in which sin and misery have ever been permitted to enter—and that they have been suffered here for moral effect and restraint upon all other planets.

It has been often objected to the gospel, that, if the universe of worlds is as extensive as modern astronomy represents, that there are all around us myriads of worlds vastly larger and more resplendent than our own; it is unreasonable to suppose that so much attention would be bestowed upon this insignificant province of Jehovah's empire, as the gospel represents—that for us God should give his son to die, when our earth, and the system of which it is a part, are as nothing compared with the innumerable orbs which fill the immensity of space. This objection rests on the supposition, that the inhabitants of all other worlds are in a similar fallen condition to us; and that they are all, therefore, in equal need of a Saviour. Were this true, it would indeed be unreasonable and incredible, that our world should be made the peculiar theatre of such divine manifestations as are brought to view in the Scriptures. But this objection really has no weight, if this is the only planet in the universe that has fallen. Now, the fact that there is no intimation given in Scripture that any other planet has sinned, or needs an atoning Saviour, and the fact that Jesus did come to seek and to save that which was lost here, is to my mind satisfactory proof, that we only, aside from the fallen angels, needed his aid. Certainly no one has a right to infer, or assume, that all other worlds are as miserable as this.

Now, if this is the only world that has rebelled against the laws of heaven, it is not unreasonable that that very special attention should be bestowed by the universal Lord of all, represented in his Word. Should some one insignificant province of a vast empire rebel against its rightful sovereign, the attention of the king, and his ministers, and his loyal subjects, universally, would very naturally and properly be directed more intently to this than any other. And should the king, knowing his power to crush them in the shortest time, first send to them, repeatedly, offers of pardon, and last of all, his son to plead with them, and bring them back, if possible, to subjection, by kindness and love, such a course would not be inconsistent or irrational. The king might see, that such a procedure would not only be adapted to exhibit his own character most conspicuously, but would be the most effectual way to endear to himself the subjects of his wide-spread empire, and thus to prevent further rebellion. After all this exhibition of kindness, it would not only be right for him to execute the law upon those who would not repent and submit, but his justice would be universally approved.

Now, we apprehend that very similar to this is the case before us. This world is the only one that has rebelled. And hence, though insignificant in comparison with the other vast provinces of the empire of Jehovah, the attention of the universal King —of his ministers, the angels—and of his loyal subjects in all other worlds, is very specially and earnestly directed hither; and here God is manifesting his love and mercy, before proceeding to the execution of the final sentence, to the wonder and admiration of the universe. All this is substantially brought to view in Scripture. Though, in the love and wisdom of God, special attention is given to us, yet the moral effect is designed for all other worlds, and is felt in far-distant regions.

In his epistle to the Ephesians, 3 : 10, the Apostle teaches, that all that has been done for our world through Jesus Christ, was "*To the intent* that now unto the *principalities* and *powers* in heavenly places," or inhabiting other worlds in the heavens, "might be known by the church the manifold wisdom of God, according to the eternal purpose which he purposed in Christ Jesus our Lord." By the manifold wisdom of God, is meant, his perfections variously and wisely manifested in the redemption of man.

In this passage it is expressly revealed that the design of God in the great love manifested to this world, is not only to save man, but to manifest or make himself known to other worlds, with a view, no doubt, to moral effect. But what effect can all this have upon them, if they have never sinned? By seeing, or hearing, through angelic ministration, his mercy and compassion shown to the rebellious here, they may learn more of the loveliness of his character, than they could otherwise know, and thus become attached more ardently to him. By knowing the miseries produced by sin here, they may see the necessity of obedience to happiness, and that it is an exceedingly evil and bitter thing to sin against the Lord. By learning that the sufferings of Jesus the Son of God, were necessary to redeem from sin, their conceptions of the dreadful nature of sin may be indefinitely increased, and thus they may be led to hate and to shun it. And finally, by seeing so many as do, turn away from the offers of heaven's mercy, and reject the gospel, and by witnessing the necessary and eternal banishment of the impenitent from God, and their consequent sufferings—they may be led exceedingly to fear sin, and to cling with undying desire to truth, love, and obedience. Thus the moral effect of the introduction of sin into our world—the redemption of Jesus—and the final misery of the *confirmed in sin*, may be to preserve all other worlds in obedience and happiness. God, we may suppose, in all worlds, governs intelligent and free agents by moral means—by motives addressed to their understandings and hearts. In the view taken, the means are adapted, and abundantly sufficient, under God, to produce the result contemplated.

I know not what effect these considerations may have upon other minds, but they tend exceedingly to satisfy and reconcile my own. Regarding this as the only rebellious world, it causes the misery, which will exist in the universe through eternal ages, to dwindle to a very small space, in comparison with the innumerable happy orbs which will continue to roll on undisturbed by sin—while that which does exist will be overruled for the universal good.

And then in respect to those who suffer—the conviction that their misery is just, that it is self-induced, and self-perpetuated, because they would not love and submit to God in his gospel, and obey his laws, will as effectually reconcile all the holy to the condemnation of the wicked, as peaceable and honest citizens are now to the imprisonment and punishment of the disturbers of the peace and order of society.

THE END.

www.ingramcontent.com/pod-product-compliance
Lightning Source LLC
LaVergne TN
LVHW020240110826
845151LV00003B/980
9781425530129